WRITING Bible 라이팅 바이블

지은이 황선원 · Stephanie Choi
펴낸이 안용백
펴낸곳 (주)넥서스

초판 1쇄 발행 2012년 2월 10일
초판 2쇄 발행 2012년 2월 15일

출판신고 1992년 4월 3일 제311-2002-2호
121-840 서울시 마포구 서교동 394-2
Tel (02)330-5500 Fax (02)330-5555
ISBN 978-89-5797-988-4   13740

저자와 출판사의 허락없이 내용의 일부를
인용하거나 발췌하는 것을 금합니다.
저자와의 협의에 따라 인지는 붙이지 않습니다.

가격은 뒤표지에 있습니다.
잘못 만들어진 책은 구입처에서 바꾸어 드립니다.

www.nexusbook.com

STEP BY STEP 라이팅의 기초✓를 만들어 가는

라이팅 바이블

황선원·Stephanie Choi 지음

여는 글 >>> Preface

언어 학습(Language Acquisition)의 단계는 통상적으로 4단계(Four Skills), 듣기(Listening), 읽기(Reading), 말하기(Speaking), 그리고 쓰기(Writing)로 구분되어지고 있다.
영어가 이 땅에 처음 도입되어 교육다운 교육이 이루어지기 시작했을 때는 읽기 위주의 교육이 대부분이었다. 잘 읽기 위해서 우리는 문장(Sentence)의 규칙(Rule)인 문법(Grammar)을 아주 열심히 배웠으며 모든 시험은 독해(Reading Comprehension)와 문법 시험(Grammar Test)이 주를 이루었다.

그러나 시간이 흐름에 따라 사회적 요구(Social Needs)가 다양해지면서 듣기(Listening)가 영어 교육의 화두(Hot Issue)가 되더니 이제는 말하기(Speaking)가 그 자리를 차지해가고 있다. 그렇다면 이제 남은 하나는 무엇인지는 분명해졌다. 바로 쓰기(Writing)인 것이다. 우리 영어 교육의 현실은 그 모든 것이 시험(Examination)에 좌우되어 왔으며 앞으로도 그럴 것이 분명하다.

TOEFL, TOEIC, TEPS, 수능 시험, 학교 시험 등의 문제가 어떤 형태로 출제되느냐에 따라 영어교육 방향과 방법이 맞춰지고 있다. 2014년부터 국가에서 주관하는 국가영어능력시험(National English Ability Test)이 새롭게 등장할 예정이다. 이 시험은 영어 학습의 4단계(Four Skills)를 모두 포함하는 발전적 시험 제도(Developed Test System)이다.

여기에서 우리에게 가장 **취약한 부분**은 바로 **쓰기**(Writing) 분야이다. 지금껏 우리는 쓰기(Writing)와 작문(Composition)을 구분하지 못해 왔다. 그래서 우리말을 영어로 옮겨 쓰는 번역(Translation)을 쓰기(Writing)로 잘못 여기고 각종의 표현 방식을 공부했다. 그러나 영어 학습의 4단계 중 하나인 쓰기(Writing)는 그것과는 전혀 다른 개념의 분야이다. 즉, **생각하고**(Thought), **창조하며**(Creation), **논리적인**(Logic) 자기 주도형 학습인 것이다.

저자는 바로 여기, **자기 주도형 학습**(Self-oriented Study)에 **중점**을 두고 본 교재를 집필하였다. 이제 여러분은 다양한 문제를 통해 생각하고, 창조하고 그리고 논리적으로 여러분의 견해를 당당하게 표현해 주길 바란다.

황선원

목차 >>> Contents

Part I — Basic Course | 8
10가지 문제 유형으로 총 64개의 문제가 제시되어 있다.
TOEIC 600점 이하, TEPS 500점 이하, 또는 TOEFL(IBT) 70점 이하, TOEFL(CBT) 180점 이하의 수준에 해당한다.

Part II — Intermediate Course | 76
10가지 문제 유형으로 총 72개의 문제가 제시되고 있다.
TOEIC 600~850점, TEPS 500점~800점, TOEFL(IBT) 70점~90점, TOEFL(CBT) 180~230의 수준에 해당한다.

Part III — Advanced Course | 152
10가지 문제 유형으로 총 58개의 문제가 제시되어 있다.
TOEIC 850점 이상, TEPS 800점 이상, 또는 TOEFL(IBT) 90점 이상, TOEFL(CBT) 230점 이상의 수준에 해당한다.

Part IV — Exercise | 220
지금까지 배운 영작 훈련으로 스토리를 만들어 보는 문제가 제시되어 있다. 난이도가 갑자기 높아졌다고 보일 수도 있지만 이 책을 착실하게 따라온 학생이라면 어렵지 않게 완성할 수 있을 것으로 확신한다.

• Sample Answers | 238

책의 특징

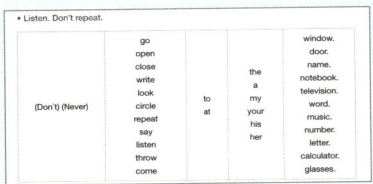

01. Sentence Completion 문장 완성
주어진 단어 Word와 구 Phrase를 연결하여 자신이 생각하는 문장을 다양하게 만들어 보는 문제 형태이다. 그러나 여기서 유의해야 할 사항은 문장 Sentence이나 단락 Paragraph은 논리적 Logical이어야 한다는 것이다. 즉 문장의 통일성 Unity과 의미의 일관성 Coherence이 중요하다.

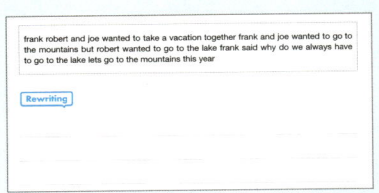

02. Sentence Rewriting 문장 재작성
주어진 단락의 각각의 단어는 모두 소문자이며 또한 구두점이 전혀 없다. 그러므로 각각의 문장이 어디서 시작되고 어디서 끝나는지를 알 수가 없다. 먼저 첫 단어의 시작을 대문자로 바꾸면 그 단어의 뜻을 쉽게 알 수 있을 것이다. 그 후 단어를 천천히 읽어 가면서 하나 하나의 문장을 만들어 간다. 주어진 단락 Paragraph은 이미 논리적으로 구성되어 있기 때문에 그 뜻을 이해하는 데 큰 어려움은 없다.

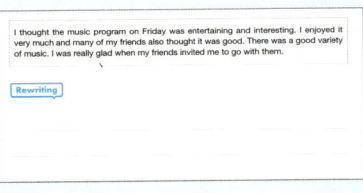

03. Transformation 문장 변형
주어진 단락 Paragraph에서 인칭대명사에 변화를 주거나 동사의 시제 Tense에 변화를 주면 그에 따른 변화가 일어난다. 문제의 지시에 따라 인칭대명사의 경우에는 주격, 소유격, 목적격 그리고 소유대명사의 형태가 변형될 것이며, 동사의 경우에는 동사의 형태나 시제에 변화가 있을 것이다. 주어진 단락 Paragraph은 논리적으로 구성되어 있기 때문에 논리성에 대한 변화는 없다.

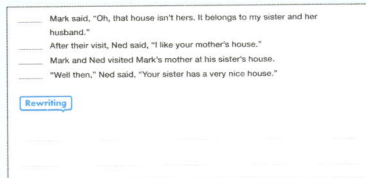

04. Sentence Ordering 문장 순서 정하기
주어진 각각의 문장을 읽고 시간순에 따라 순서를 정한 후 그 순서를 주어진 문장 왼쪽에 기입한다. 그리고 순서가 다 정해지면 순서에 따라 단락 Paragraph을 완성한다. 이러한 형태의 문제는 시간순 방식 Time Sequence에 따른 논리성이 핵심이다.

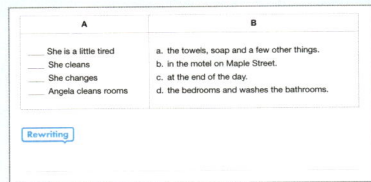

05. Matching 연결
A난 Column A과 B난 Column B에 주어진 구 Pharse와 절 Clauses을 서로 연결하여 논리성 Logic을 갖춘 뒤 시간순 방식 Time Sequence 혹은 논리적 방식 Logical Ordering을 적용시켜 합리적인 지문을 완성시켜 나가는 문제 형태이다. A난 Column A에 주어진 번호 1, 2, 3…옆 밑줄 친 부분에 B난 Column B의 문자 a, b, c…를 선택하여 기입한 후 단락을 완성한다.

>>> features

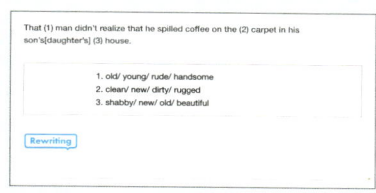

06. Expansion 문장 확장

주어진 문장에 보기 속의 어휘를 삽입시켜 확장시켜 나가는 형태의 문제이다. 각각의 번호에 자신이 생각하는 어휘를 삽입하여 글을 창조하되 반드시 논리적으로 일치 Agreement해야 한다.

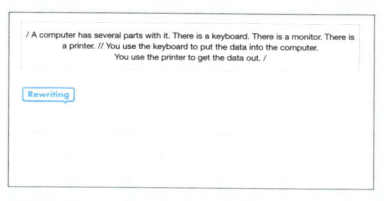

07. Formulation 문장 재구성

각각의 문장을 통해 단락 전체를 보다 간결 Simple하고 세련 Refined되게 만드는 문제 형태이다. 여기에 주로 사용되는 방법은 생략법 Ellipsis과 공통 관계 Common Relations이다. 즉 공통된 주어를 활용하며, 열거 Listing표시의 and를 ' , '로 처리하는 방식 등이 있다. 또한 관계대명사를 비롯하여 다양한 접속사를 활용하여 시간, 원인이나 이유, 조건 양보 표현을 추가함으로써 주어진 단락의 내용을 자신의 표현 방식으로 다듬어 글을 재구성 Paraphrasing해 본다.

08. Dictation 받아쓰기

먼저 주어진 문제의 단락을 듣는다. 자신의 학습 능력에 따라 한 번 혹은 두 번 들을 수 있다. 듣고 난 후 주어진 단어를 활용하여 들었던 문장을 원문에 충실하게 작성한다. 무엇보다 중요한 것은 원문의 전반적 내용이 무엇인지를 파악하는 것이다. 박스에 나와 있는 번호는 원문의 문장 순서와 일치하며 주어진 단어는 문장에 나와 있는 단어이다.

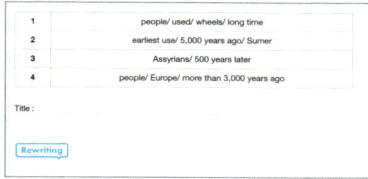

09. Guided Writing 문장 유도

먼저 주어진 문제의 지문을 듣는다. 자신의 학습 능력에 따라 혹은 교사의 지시에 따라 횟수를 조절할 수 있다. 듣고 난 후 박스 안에 주어진 어휘를 이용하여 들었던 문장을 재작성해 본다. 무엇보다 중요한 것은 원문의 전반적 내용이 무엇인지를 파악하는 것이 중요하다. 받아쓰기 Dictation와 다른 점은 각각의 문장이 원문과는 다르게 쉽게 바꿔쓰기 Paraphrasing 된다는 사실이다. 박스에 주어진 번호는 원문의 문장 순서와 일치한다.

10. Summary 요약

먼저 주어진 문제의 단락을 읽은 후 주어진 단어를 활용하여 문장을 다시 구성 Paraphrasing한다. 무엇보다 중요한 것은 원문의 전반적 내용을 파악하는 것이다. 그러므로 이해하고, 생각하고, 주어진 단어를 활용하여 단락의 내용을 자신의 표현 방식으로 요약한다.

Part I

Basic Course

Make perfect sentences using the words in the box. (Answers will vary.)

> **Point**
> 긍정 명령문과 부정 명령문을 전치사와 결합하여 완성한다. 그러나 타동사의 경우에는 전치사 없이 목적어를 취할 수 있기 때문에 전치사와 결합할 때 유의하며 학습한다. 문장은 1형식과 3형식이다.

• Listen. Don't repeat.

| (Don't) (Never) | go
open
close
write
look
circle
repeat
say
listen
throw
come | to
at | the
a
my
your
his
her | window.
door.
name.
notebook.
television.
word.
music.
number.
letter.
calculator.
glasses. |

Writing   *ex* Go to the window.

1.

2.

3.

4.

5.

Make perfect sentences using the words in the box. (Answers will vary.)

Point

의문 대명사 what을 이용한 의문문에 대한 답으로 지시 대명사 this, that, it을 이용한 서술문을 완성한다. 그리고 명사 앞에 오는 관사 a와 소유격 형용사를 학습한다. 문장은 2형식이다.

- What is this? = What's this?
- What is that? = What's that?
- What is it? = What's it?

This That It	is	a my your her his	picture. letter. word. number. lab. classroom. watch. dictionary.

Writing   *ex* This is a picture.

1.

2.

3.

4.

5.

Make perfect sentences using the words in the box. (Answers will vary.)

Point

What 의문문에 대한 답으로 인칭 대명사 I, you, he, she 그리고 인칭 고유 대명사를 이용하여 의문문에 대한 답을 완성한다. What은 직업을 묻는다. 그리고 명사 앞에 부정관사 a와 an의 사용에 유의해야 한다. 문장은 2형식이다.

- What am I?
- What are you?
- What is she[he]?
- What is Paul[Jane]?

I You He She Paul Jane	am are is	(not)	a an	doctor. teacher. mechanic. cook. musician. artist. computer programmer. babysitter. taxi driver.

Writing   ex I am a doctor.

1.

2.

3.

4.

5.

Make perfect sentences using the words in the box. (Answers will vary.)

Point

Yes/No 의문문에 대한 답을 완성한다. 인칭에 따른 be동사의 선택과 명사의 발음에 따른 부정관사 a와 an의 선택에 유의해야 한다. Not은 선택이며 문장은 2형식이다.

- Am I a worker?
- Are you a nurse?
- Is he[she] a professor?

| Yes,
No, | I
you
he
she
Paula
Mark | am
are
is | (not) | a
an | worker.
nurse.
professor.
actress.
model.
businessman.
policeman.
editor.
gardener. |

Writing *ex* No, I am not a model.

1.

2.

3.

4.

5.

Make perfect sentences using the words in the box. (Answers will vary.)

Point

먼저 '관사+명사' 그리고 '소유격 형용사+명사'를 결합시켜 주어를 만든 후, 단수와 복수에 따른 be동사를 선택한다. 그 다음 '전치사+명사'의 전치사구를 만든 후 하나의 완벽한 문장을 완성한다. 문장은 1형식이며 여기서 be동사의 의미는 '~에 있다'이다.

- The cup is on the table.
- My socks are under the bed.
- Your ring is in my pocket.

| The
A(n)
My
Your
His
Her
Our
Their | socks
clock(s)
necklace(s)
pillow(s)
book(s)
bicycle(s)
television(s)
key(s)
picture(s) | is
are | (not) | in
at
on
inside
outside
under | my
your
his
her
the
a | pocket.
table.
house.
box.
desk.
wall.
lab.
bedroom.
living room.
kitchen. |

Writing

ex Her key is on the desk.

1. _____
2. _____
3. _____
4. _____
5. _____

14 • Writing Bible

Make perfect sentences using the words in the box. (Answers will vary.)

> **Point**
>
> 신체와 감정 상태를 나타내는 형용사를 활용하여 문장을 완성한다. 주어에 따른 be동사의 선택에 유의하며 not과 very는 선택이다. 문장은 2형식이며 여기서 be동사의 의미는 '~이다'이다.

- Kathy is very happy.
- Fred is not very sick.
- The children are not satisfied.

I You He She Mr. Smith Ms. Creamer Fred Kathy The students	am are is	(not)	(very)	happy. sick. hot. cold. satisfied. young. old. angry. scared. thirsty. embarrassed. relieved.

Writing   *ex* I am not very angry.

1. _____

2. _____

3. _____

4. _____

5. _____

Rewrite the paragraph. Put in capital letters, apostrophes, question marks and periods, if necessary.

Point

문장의 시작과 끝을 의미로 찾은 후 마침표(period)와 대문자(capital letter)를 활용하여 문장을 다시 구성한다. 그리고 콤마(comma)와 아포스트로피(apostrophe) 그리고 물음표(question mark)를 이용하여 문장을 완성한다. 대부분의 문장은 1형식, 2형식 그리고 3형식이다.

do you like to walk i do its good for you all you need is good shoes take a friend with you you can talk and walk at the same time walk together every day youll feel good

Rewriting

Put these sentences in order. Then rewrite the sentences as one paragraph.

Point

논리순(logical order) 방식에 따라 순서에 맞게 번호를 적은 후 의미의 일관성(coherence)과 통일성(unity)을 갖춘 완성된 단락(complete paragraph)을 작성한다. 시간을 나타내는 부사 then과 first 등에 유의한다. 자동판매기(vendimg machine) 사용법을 참고해 보자. 문장은 3형식, 4형식(tell동사의 용법) 그리고 5형식(get동사의 용법)이다.

_____ Put your money in the slot.
_____ Get it out.
_____ Please tell me how to operate this machine.
_____ Push the button.
_____ Get the exact change.

Rewriting

Match the phrases/clauses in column A with those in column B to form sentences. Then rewrite the sentences in order as one paragraph.

> **Point**
>
> column A와 어울리는 표현을 column B에서 찾아 연결한 후 시간순(time order) 그리고 논리순(logical order) 방식에 따라 순서를 정한다. 의미의 일관성(coherence)과 통일성(unity)을 갖춘 완성된 단락(complete paragraph)을 작성한다. 문장은 1형식, 2형식 그리고 3형식이다.

A	B
____ He got some change and	a. but the line was busy.
____ Yesterday, Tim wanted to	b. make a long distance call.
____ He dialed the number,	c. went to the pay phone.

Rewriting

Read the paragraph; then choose a word for each number. Add the words to the paragraph and rewrite it on the lines below. (Answers will vary.)

Point

박스 안에 주어진 단어 중 적절한 단어를 번호에 맞게 선택한 후 주어진 문장에 추가하여 좀 더 길고 완벽한 문장을 만드는 학습이다. 이때 주의해야 할 사항은 의미의 일관성(coherence)이다. 먼저 박스 안에 주어진 단어의 의미가 파악되어야 한다. 문장은 2형식이며 to 부정사는 부사적 용법으로 '이유'를 나타낸다.

They were (1) to see each other after (2) years. They were (3).

1. happy/ confused/ surprised/ excited
2. many/ several/ a few/ a lot of
3. pleased/ embarrassed/ shocked/ ashamed

Rewriting

011

Make perfect sentences using the words in the box. (Answers will vary.)

> **Point**
>
> 독립된 두 개의 문장을 만들어 보는데 두 문장 사이에는 의미의 일관성(coherence)이 있어야 한다. 즉, 보어로 사용된 형용사와 전치사구의 상관성(correlation)에 유의해서 두 문장을 완성한다. 문장은 1형식과 2형식이다.

- The reporter is hurt. She is in her bedroom.

The	teller painter lawyer reporter	is	comfortable. lonely. sick. hurt.	He She	is	in	his her	cafeteria. swimming pool. house. bedroom.
							the	hospital. gymnasium.
	waiters models florists players	are	in love. uncomfortable. excited. happy.	They	are		their	clinic. shopping mall.

Writing   *ex* The painter is sick. He is in the hospital.

1.
2.
3.
4.
5.

Make perfect sentences using the words in the box. (Answers will vary.)

Point

주어의 수(단수, 복수)에 따른 동사의 일치에 유의한다. 다양한 음식을 목적어로 선택하되 'for+명사'의 전치사구와 의미상 동떨어지지 않도록 유의한다. 예를 들면, rice for snack은 어색한 표현이 될 것이다. 문장은 3형식이다.

• The clerk eats eggs for breakfast.

The courier(s) The janitor(s) The clerk(s) The writer(s) The announcer(s) The travel agent(s) The babysitter(s)	eat(s)	(a)	rice cheese-sandwich(es) fruit pork chickenburger(s) bread beefburger(s) toast(s)	for	lunch. dinner. breakfast. their snack. every meal.

Writing   *ex* The writer eats fruit for lunch.

1.
2.
3.
4.
5.

Rewrite the paragraph. Put in capital letters, apostrophes, commas, quotation marks, question marks, exclamation marks and periods, if necessary.

Point

문장의 시작과 끝을 의미로 찾은 후 마침표(period)와 대문자(capital letter)를 활용하여 문장을 다시 구성한다. 그리고 콤마(comma), 아포스트로피(apostrophe), 물음표(question mark), 따옴표(quotation mark) 그리고 느낌표(exclamation mark)를 이용하여 문장을 완성한다. 대부분의 문장은 1형식과 3형식이다.

frank robert and joe wanted to take a vacation together frank and joe wanted to go to the mountains but robert wanted to go to the lake frank said why do we always have to go to the lake lets go to the mountains this year

Rewriting

Number the sentences in the correct time sequence. Then rewrite the sentences as a complete paragraph.

> **Point**
>
> 시간순(time order) 방식에 따라 순서에 맞게 번호를 적은 후 의미의 일관성(coherence)과 통일성(unity)을 갖춘 완성된 단락(complete paragraph)을 작성한다. 동사의 시제와 시간 표시의 단어에 유의해야 한다. 문장은 1형식과 3형식이다.

_____ Mark said, "At your house, Karen. We studied for the last test at mine."

_____ Karen said, "Okay, Mark. Your house or mine?"

_____ Mark and Karen are in the same Spanish class.

_____ Mark said, "Karen, let's study for the test together."

Rewriting

Match the phrases/clauses in column A with those in column B to form sentences. Then rewrite the sentences in order as one paragraph.

Point

column A와 어울리는 표현을 column B에서 찾아 연결한 후 시간순(time order) 그리고 논리순(logical order) 방식에 따라 순서를 정한다. 의미의 일관성(coherence)과 통일성(unity)을 갖춘 완성된 단락(complete paragraph)을 작성한다. 문장은 1형식, 2형식 그리고 3형식이다.

A	B
____ They hope to	a. losing the baggage.
____ They apologized for	b. they won't find it at all.
____ Mike is upset	c. because the airline lost his baggage.
____ He's worried that	d. find it by tomorrow.

Rewriting

Read the paragraph; then choose a word for each number. Add the words to the paragraph and rewrite it on the lines below. (Answers will vary.)

Point

박스 안에 주어진 단어 중 적절한 단어를 번호에 맞게 선택한 후 주어진 문장에 추가하여 좀 더 길고 완벽한 문장을 만드는 학습이다. 이때 주의해야 할 사항은 의미의 일관성(coherence)이다. 먼저 박스 안에 주어진 단어의 의미가 파악되어야 한다. 문장은 부사구를 포함한 2형식이다.

Marty was very (1) when the (2) was (3).

> 1. angry/ upset/ happy
> 2. vending machine/ snack bar/ coffee shop
> 3. out of food/ out of order/ of good service

Rewriting

Read the paragraph. Then write the summary of the paragraph with the help of words and phrases in the box. (Summaries will vary.)

> **Point**
>
> 먼저 주어진 단락을 주의깊게 읽는다. 그리고 박스 안에 주어진 단어를 사용하여 읽었던 단락을 요약(summary)하여 요약문을 작성한다. 요약문은 1개의 문장으로 완성한다. 문장은 2형식이다. 단락을 읽을 때는 먼저 의미가 파악되어야 하며, 박스 속에 주어진 단어를 연결하여 문장을 만들 때는 문장의 통일성(unity)에 유의해야 한다. 세련된 문장을 작성하기 위해서 공통 관계와 생략법 등을 최대한 활용하면서 문법을 바르게 적용해야 한다. 또한 콤마(comma)와 물음표(question mark), 마침표(period), 그리고 대문자(capital letter) 등 구두점(punctuation) 사용에 유의한다.

Soccer is a game that almost everyone who is in good physical shape can play. In basketball, most of the players are tall. In football, many of the players are heavy and very strong. Soccer is different. A player who is fast can do well in a soccer game. He doesn't need to be tall, heavy, or strong.

speed/ size/ thing/ that/ important/ soccer/ player

Summary:

Topic:

Main idea:

Read the paragraph. Then write the summary of the paragraph with the help of words and phrases in the box. (Summaries will vary.)

> **Point**
>
> 먼저 주어진 단락을 주의깊게 읽는다. 그리고 박스 안에 주어진 단어를 사용하여 읽었던 단락을 요약(summary)하여 요약문을 작성한다. 요약문은 1개의 문장으로 완성한다. 문장은 3형식이다. 단락을 읽을 때는 먼저 의미가 파악되어야 하며, 박스 속에 주어진 단어를 연결하여 문장을 만들 때는 문장의 통일성(unity)에 유의해야 한다. 세련된 문장을 작성하기 위해서 공통 관계와 생략법 등을 최대한 활용하면서 문법적으로 바른 문장을 작성해야 한다. 또한 콤마(comma)와 물음표(question mark), 마침표(period), 그리고 대문자(capital letter) 등 구두점(punctuation) 사용에 유의한다.

Keith knows how to study for a test. She starts getting ready for it early. She reviews the lessons in the textbook first. Next she looks at her notebook and memorizes the important things in it. After that, she usually writes questions and practices answering them. She always makes a good grade on a test.

Keith/ makes/ a good grade/ test/ because/ how/ study

Summary:

Topic:

Main idea:

Read the paragraph. Then write the summary of the paragraph with the help of words and phrases in the box. (Summaries will vary.)

> **Point**
>
> 먼저 주어진 단락을 주의깊게 읽는다. 그리고 박스 안에 주어진 단어를 사용하여 읽었던 단락을 요약(summary)하여 요약문을 작성한다. 요약문은 1개의 문장으로 완성한다. 문장은 3형식이다. 단락을 읽을 때는 먼저 의미가 파악되어야 하며, 박스 속에 주어진 단어를 연결하여 문장을 만들 때는 문장의 통일성(unity)에 유의해야 한다. 세련된 문장을 작성하기 위해서 공통 관계와 생략법 등을 최대한 활용하면서 문법을 바르게 적용해야 한다. 또한 콤마(comma)와 물음표(question mark), 마침표(period), 그리고 대문자(capital letter) 등 구두점(punctuation) 사용에 유의한다.

When an old man got on the bus, he realized that it was very crowded. He thought, "Oh, no! I'll have to stand up, and I'm very tired." Then a young man who saw him stood and said, "Please sit down here, sir." The old man thanked the young man, and sat down.

| old/ who/ crowded/ didn't have to/ because/ polite/ gave/ seat |

Summary:

Make questions using the words in the box. (Answers will vary.)

> **Point**
>
> 의문사 Where와 be동사를 활용하여 의문문을 완성한다. 인칭 대명사와 인칭 고유 대명사 앞에는 관사나 소유격 형용사를 쓸 수 없음에 유의한다. 문장은 1형식이다.

- Where is the map?
- Where are you?

Where	are is	my your his her the	Bill? book(s)? glasses? auditorium(s)? cafeteria(s)? library(-ies)? you? gym(s)? pay phone(s)? lotion(s)?

Writing *ex* Where are you?

1.
2.
3.
4.
5.

Make questions using the words in the box. (Answers will vary.)

> **Point**
>
> 먼저 의문 형용사 Whose를 활용한 단수 혹은 복수 의문문을 만든 뒤에 질문에 대한 답을 완성한다. 수(단수, 복수)의 일치에 유의하면서 다양한 문장을 만든다. Whose는 뒤에 나오는 명사를 수식하며 문장은 2형식이다.

- Whose money is this?
- This is my money.

Whose	jacket(s) pants money friend(s) television(s) guitar(s) violin(s) computer(s) smart phone(s)	is are	this? that? these? those? they?

Writing   *ex* Whose violin is that?

1. _____

2. _____

3. _____

4. _____

5. _____

This That It These Those They	are is	my your his her our their	jacket(s). pants. money. friend(s). television(s). guitar(s). violin(s). computer(s). smart phone(s).

Writing   *ex* That is my violin.

1.
2.
3.
4.
5.

Rewrite the paragraph and put in capital letters, apostrophes and periods, if necessary.

Point

문장의 시작과 끝을 의미로 찾은 후 마침표(period)와 대문자(capital letter)를 활용하여 문장을 다시 구성한다. 그리고 아포스트로피(apostrophe)를 이용하여 문장을 완성한다. 대부분의 문장은 1형식과 3형식이다.

> linda watched tv for two hours next she took a long shower she washed her hair she dried her body and hair with a clean towel then a friend called linda on the phone they will have a korean test tomorrow linda didnt study for the test

Rewriting

Read the paragraph. Change 'I' to 'he.' Underline other parts of the paragraph that need changing. Rewrite the changed paragraph.

Point

1인칭 주어 I를 3인칭 주어 he로 바꾸어 각각의 문장을 다시 작성한다. 먼저 전환이 필요한 단어에 밑줄을 긋는다. 주어의 변경에 따라 소유격 my는 his로, 목적격 me는 him으로 전환한다. 학습이 끝나면 I를 you, she, they 등으로 바꿔 학습한다. 문장은 1형식(There 구문)과 3형식이다.

I thought the music program on Friday was entertaining and interesting. I enjoyed it very much and many of my friends also thought it was good. There was a good variety of music. I was really glad when my friends invited me to go with them.

Rewriting

Number the sentences in the correct time sequence. Then rewrite the sentences as a complete paragraph.

Point

시간순(time order) 방식과 논리순(logical order) 방식에 따라 순서에 맞게 번호를 적은 후 의미의 일관성(coherence)과 통일성(unity)을 갖춘 완성된 단락(complete paragraph)을 작성한다. 시간 표시의 전치사 after에 유의한다. 문장은 1형식, 2형식 그리고 3형식이다.

_____ Mark said, "Oh, that house isn't hers. It belongs to my sister and her husband."

_____ After their visit, Ned said, "I like your mother's house."

_____ Mark and Ned visited Mark's mother at his sister's house.

_____ "Well then," Ned said, "Your sister has a very nice house."

Rewriting

Match the phrases/clauses in column A with those in column B to form sentences. Then rewrite the sentences in order as one paragraph.

> **Point**
>
> column A와 어울리는 표현을 column B에서 찾아 연결한 후 시간순(time order) 그리고 논리순(logical order) 방식에 따라 순서를 정한다. 의미의 일관성(coherence)과 통일성(unity)을 갖춘 완성된 단락(complete paragraph)을 작성한다. 문장은 2형식과 3형식이다.

A	B
____ She is a little tired ____ She cleans ____ She changes ____ Angela cleans rooms	a. the towels, soap and a few other things. b. in the motel on Maple Street. c. at the end of the day. d. the bedrooms and washes the bathrooms.

Rewriting

Read the paragraph; then choose a word for each number. Add the words to the paragraph and rewrite it on the lines below. (Answers will vary.)

Point

박스 안에 주어진 단어 중 적절한 단어를 번호에 맞게 선택한 후 주어진 문장에 추가하여 좀 더 길고 완벽한 문장을 만드는 학습이다. 이때 주의해야 할 사항은 의미의 일관성(coherence)이다. 먼저 박스 안에 주어진 단어의 의미가 파악되어야 한다. 문장은 전치사구를 동반한 3형식이다.

The (1) woman met the (2) sailor at a (3) restaurant.

1. beautiful/ smiling/ weeping/ furious
2. nice/ handsome/ miserable/ smug
3. small/ quiet/ shabby/ crowded

Rewriting

Read the paragraph. Then write the summary of the paragraph with the help of words and phrases in the boxes. (Summaries will vary.)

> **Point**
>
> 먼저 주어진 단락을 주의깊게 읽는다. 그리고 박스 안에 주어진 단어를 사용하여 읽었던 단락을 요약(summary)하여 요약문을 작성한다. 요약문은 2개의 문장으로 완성한다. 문장은 3형식이다. 단락을 읽을 때는 먼저 의미가 파악되어야 하며, 박스 속에 주어진 단어를 연결하여 문장을 만들 때는 문장의 통일성(unity)에 유의해야 한다. 세련된 문장을 작성하기 위해서 공통 관계와 생략법 등을 최대한 활용하면서 문법을 바르게 적용해야 한다. 또한 콤마(comma)와 물음표(question mark), 마침표(period), 그리고 대문자(capital letter) 등 구두점(punctuation) 사용에 유의한다.

Brad reads and collects magazines. He buys his magazines from his favorite book store. He reads each one from front to back. Then he puts them on a shelf and writes the name, date and shelf number in a notebook. When Brad wants a magazine, he can always find it.

1	Brad/ and/ magazines
2	each/ from/ to
3	can/ find/ one/ in his collection/ because of/ way/ keeps

Summary:

Topic:

Main idea:

Make questions using the words in the box. (Answers will vary.)

Point

먼저 의문대명사 What을 이용한 진행형 의문문(progressive question)을 만든다. 주어에 대한 동사의 일치와 주어, 동사, 그리고 동사에 따른 전치사의 선택에 유의하여 합리적인 문장을 완성한다. 문장은 1형식과 3형식이다.

- What are you doing?
- I'm reading.

What	am are is	I you Rick Janet they the children	doing?

Writing

ex What is Rick doing?

1.
2.
3.
4.
5.

Match the phrases/clauses in column A with those in column B to form sentences. Then rewrite the sentences in order as one paragraph.

> **Point**
>
> column A와 어울리는 표현을 column B에서 찾아 연결한 후 시간순(time order) 그리고 논리순(logical order) 방식에 따라 순서를 정한다. 의미의 일관성(coherence)과 통일성(unity)을 갖춘 완성된 단락(complete paragraph)을 작성한다. 문장은 1형식과 2형식 그리고 3형식이다.

A	B
____ Chris was	a. hangers in the closet.
____ There were no	b. very angry.
____ He couldn't	c. an old motel.
____ Chris checked in at	d. hang up his clothes.

Rewriting

Rewrite the paragraph and put in capital letters, apostrophes and periods, if necessary.

Point

문장의 시작과 끝을 의미로 찾은 후 마침표(period)와 대문자(capital letter)를 활용하여 문장을 다시 구성한다. 그리고 아포스트로피(apostrophe)를 이용하여 문장을 완성한다. 대부분의 문장은 1형식, 2형식 그리고 3형식이다.

paula hurt her leg at a soccer game she didnt go to the doctor that day her leg was very sore she went to bed and took medicine the next day her leg was very sore again she then went to the doctors office her leg is well now

Rewriting

Read the paragraph. Then write the summary of the paragraph with the help of words and phrases in the boxes. (Summaries will vary.)

> **Point**
>
> 먼저 주어진 단락을 주의깊게 읽는다. 그리고 박스 안에 주어진 단어를 사용하여 읽었던 단락을 요약(summary)하여 요약문을 작성한다. 요약문은 2개의 문장으로 완성한다. 문장은 2형식과 3형식이다. 단락을 읽을 때는 먼저 의미가 파악되어야 하며, 박스 속에 주어진 단어를 연결하여 문장을 만들 때는 문장의 통일성(unity)에 유의해야 한다. 세련된 문장을 작성하기 위해서 공통 관계와 생략법 등을 최대한 활용하면서 문법을 바르게 적용해야 한다. 또한 콤마(comma)와 물음표(question mark), 마침표(period), 그리고 대문자(capital letter) 등 구두점(punctuation) 사용에 유의한다.

Luke wanted to do his laundry, but he needed some detergent. He went to a vending machine. He got some change and put it in the slot. Luke found it out of order. He had to go back to his room with his dirty clothes.

1	Luke/ do/ laundry/ because/ not/ detergent
2	vending machine/ out of order/ too

Summary:

Topic:

Main idea:

Combine the ideas into some sentences. And then rewrite a paragraph with the new sentences. (Rewritings will vary.)

Point

공통 관계(common relation)와 생략(ellipsis)법을 적용하여 문장을 간소화한다. 먼저 각각의 문장을 읽고 이해한 후 주어와 동사 그리고 목적어의 공통 관계를 파악한다. 그리고 생략법에 따라 문장을 결합한다. 무엇보다 문장의 통일성(unity)에 유의해야 한다. 필요한 경우에 적절한 접속사, 관계 대명사, 전치사, (대)명사, (대)동사, 조동사 그리고 형용사나 부사 등을 사용하여 단락 전체의 의미를 좀 더 명확하게 한다. 그러나 단락의 일관성(coherence)은 유지해야 한다. "/ /" 속에 포함된 문장들을 결합시켜 하나의 문장으로 다시 작성하여 단락을 완성한다. 문장은 1형식과 3형식이다.

/ Mr. Black works in an office. He keys data into a computer. // He prints the information. He makes copies of it for his boss. His boss is Mr. Green. /

Rewriting

Read the paragraph; then choose a word for each number. Add the words to the paragraph and rewrite it on the lines below. (Answers will vary.)

Point

박스 안에 주어진 단어 중 적절한 단어를 번호에 맞게 선택한 후 주어진 문장에 추가하여 좀 더 길고 완벽한 문장을 만드는 학습이다. 이때 주의해야 할 사항은 의미의 일관성(coherence)이다. 먼저 박스 안에 주어진 단어의 의미가 파악되어야 한다. 문장은 전치사구를 동반한 3형식이다.

The (1) woman picked up the (2) box and put it in her (3) car.

1. tall/ beautiful/ slender/ plump
2. heavy/ square/ light/ old
3. red/ dirty/ clean/ expensive

Rewriting

Match the phrases/clauses in column A with those in column B to form sentences. Then rewrite the sentences in order as one paragraph.

> **Point**
>
> column A와 어울리는 표현을 column B에서 찾아 연결한 후 시간순(time order) 그리고 논리순(logical order) 방식에 따라 순서를 정한다. 의미의 일관성(coherence)과 통일성(unity)을 갖춘 완성된 단락(complete paragraph)을 작성한다. 문장은 1형식과 3형식이다.

A	B
____ 1. She'll just	a. write a check.
____ 2. Today, she got her checks	b. opened a checking account.
____ 3. Now she doesn't need	c. in the mail.
____ 4. Last week, Mary went to the bank and	d. to take money with her.

Rewriting

Read the paragraph. Change the present tense to past tense. Underline the parts of the paragraph that need changing. Rewrite the changed paragraph.

Point

현재시제(present tense)를 과거시제(past tense)로 바꿔 각각의 문장을 다시 작성한다. 먼저 전환이 필요한 단어에 밑줄을 긋는다. 가능한 경우 주어 I를 you, he, she 그리고 they 등으로 바꿔 학습한다. 문장의 형식은 2형식과 3형식이다.

I'm really excited. I have a ticket for the last baseball game of the year. I'm sure it's going to be great! Both teams are strong. I expect to see a lot of people at the stadium. I'm not worried because I have reservations, and I know I have a good ticket.

Rewriting

Number the sentences in the correct time sequence. Then rewrite the sentences as a complete paragraph.

> **Point**
>
> 시간순(time order) 방식에 따라 순서에 맞게 번호를 적은 후 의미의 일관성(coherence)과 통일성(unity)을 갖춘 완성된 단락(complete paragraph)을 작성한다. 동사의 시제와 시간 표시의 부사구, 접속사 등에 유의해야 한다. 문장은 1형식, 2형식 그리고 3형식이다.

_____ Today he must pack his suitcases.
_____ Henry called the travel agency and made a reservation last week.
_____ After he packs, he'll be ready for his vacation.
_____ Yesterday he went there and picked up his ticket.

Rewriting

Read the paragraph; then choose a word for each number. Add the words to the paragraph and rewrite it on the lines below. (Answers will vary.)

Point

박스 안에 주어진 단어 중 적절한 단어를 번호에 맞게 선택한 후 주어진 문장에 추가하여 좀 더 길고 완벽한 문장을 만드는 학습이다. 이때 주의해야 할 사항은 의미의 일관성(coherence)이다. 먼저 박스 안에 주어진 단어의 의미가 파악되어야 한다. 문장은 전치사구를 동반한 3형식이다.

The (1) hostess cut the (2) pie and put it on the (3) plate.

1. young/ tired/ upset/ pretty
2. hot/ apple/ delicious/ chocolate
3. clean/ glass/ white/ antique

Rewriting

Combine the ideas into some sentences. And then rewrite a paragraph with the new setences.(Rewritings will vary.)

Point

공통 관계(common relation)와 생략(ellipsis)법을 적용하여 문장을 간소화한다. 먼저 각각의 문장을 읽고 이해한 후 주어와 동사 그리고 목적어의 공통 관계를 파악한다. 그리고 생략법에 따라 문장을 결합한다. 무엇보다 문장의 통일성(unity)에 유의해야 한다. 필요한 경우에 적절한 접속사, 관계 대명사, 전치사, (대)명사, (대)동사, 조동사 그리고 형용사나 부사 등을 사용하여 단락 전체의 의미를 좀 더 명확하게 한다. 그러나 단락의 일관성(coherence)은 유지해야 한다. "/ /" 속에 포함된 문장들을 결합시켜 하나의 문장으로 다시 작성하여 단락을 완성한다. 문장은 2형식과 3형식이다.

/ Susan became frightened. The bald, elderly man in the park sat down beside her. He started to speak. // He had a dishonest face. She didn't trust him. /

Rewriting

Read the paragraph. Then write the summary of the paragraph with the help of words and phrases in the boxes. (Summaries will vary.)

> **Point**
>
> 먼저 주어진 단락을 주의깊게 읽는다. 그리고 박스 안에 주어진 단어를 사용하여 읽었던 단락을 요약(summary)하여 요약문을 작성한다. 요약문은 2개의 문장으로 완성한다. 문장은 2형식과 3형식이다. 단락을 읽을 때는 먼저 의미가 파악되어야 하며, 박스 속에 주어진 단어를 연결하여 문장을 만들 때는 문장의 통일성(unity)에 유의해야 한다. 세련된 문장을 작성하기 위해서 공통 관계와 생략법 등을 최대한 활용하면서 문법을 바르게 적용해야 한다. 필요할 때는 콤마(comma)와 물음표(question mark), 마침표(period), 그리고 대문자(capital letter) 등 구두점(punctuation)을 사용한다.

Janet is a businesswoman. She works for a magazine. Her work is difficult, but she's good at her job. She wants to keep it, so she works very hard.

1	Janet/ businesswoman/ who/ magazine
2	has to/ hard/ because/ wants/ keep

Summary:

Read the paragraph. Then write the summary of the paragraph with the help of words and phrases in the boxes. (Summaries will vary.)

> **Point**
>
> 먼저 주어진 단락을 주의깊게 읽는다. 그리고 박스 안에 주어진 단어를 사용하여 읽었던 단락을 요약(summary)하여 요약문을 작성한다. 요약문은 2개의 문장으로 완성한다. 문장은 1형식과 2형식이다. 단락을 읽을 때는 먼저 의미가 파악되어야 하며, 박스 속에 주어진 단어를 연결하여 문장을 만들 때는 문장의 통일성(unity)에 유의해야 한다. 세련된 문장을 작성하기 위해서 공통 관계와 생략법 등을 최대한 활용하면서 문법을 바르게 적용해야 한다. 또한 콤마(comma)와 물음표(question mark), 마침표(period), 그리고 대문자(capital letter) 등 구두점(punctuation) 사용에 유의한다.

When the weather stays very cold for a long time, large pieces of ice cover parts of the world. These big pieces of ice move and break mountains and trees. They push the earth and the mountains to other places. They change the land and the way it looks.

1	pieces/ cover/ parts/ stays/ long time
2	ice/ change/ land/ and/ way/ looks

Summary:

Topic:

Main idea:

Listen to the paragraph. And dictate a paragraph you listened to using words and the phrases in the box.

Point

먼저 들려주는 지문을 주의깊게 듣는다. 그리고 박스 안에 주어진 단어를 이용하여 들었던 지문과 같은 지문을 작성한다. 지문을 들을 때는 먼저 의미가 파악되어야 하며, 박스 속에 주어진 단어를 연결하여 문장을 만들 때는 문장의 통일성(unity)에 유의한다. 특히 들을 때 잘 들리지 않는 관사, 조동사 will, 전치사 to와 in 등에 유의하여 문법적으로 바른 문장을 작성해야 한다. 또한 콤마(comma)와 물음표(question mark), 마침표(period), 그리고 대문자(capital letter) 등 구두점(punctuation) 사용에 유의한다.

---

morning/ Susan/ big breakfast/ eggs/ slice/ bread/ banana/ carrot juice/ a big cup of/ says/ ready/ work/ after

---

Writing

Read the paragraph; then choose a word for each number. Add the words to the paragraph and rewrite it on the lines below. (Answers will vary.)

Point

박스 안에 주어진 단어 중 적절한 단어를 번호에 맞게 선택한 후 주어진 문장에 추가하여 좀 더 길고 완벽한 문장을 만드는 학습이다. 이때 주의해야 할 사항은 의미의 일관성(coherence)이다. 먼저 박스 안에 주어진 단어의 의미가 파악되어야 한다. 문장은 전치사구를 동반한 3형식이다.

Mr. Brown rented a(n) (1) apartment with a (2) couch and a (3) bookcase.

1. big/ new/ expensive/ small
2. beautiful/ blue/ huge/ little
3. cheap/ big/ heavy/ light

Rewriting

Number the sentences in the correct time sequence. Then rewrite the sentences as a complete paragraph.

Point

시간순(time order) 방식에 따라 순서에 맞게 번호를 적은 후 의미의 일관성(coherence)과 통일성(unity)을 갖춘 완성된 단락(complete paragraph)을 작성한다. 시간 표시의 전치사 after에 유의해야 한다. 문장은 1형식과 3형식이다.

_____ Jane and Sara went to the gym.
_____ Sara said, "Let's take a shower."
_____ After the game, Jane said, "I'm hot!"
_____ They played a game of table-tennis there.
_____ After their showers, they went to the cafeteria near the gym.

Rewriting

Match the phrases/clauses in column A with those in column B to form sentences. Then rewrite the sentences in order as one paragraph.

Point

column A와 어울리는 표현을 column B에서 찾아 연결한 후 시간순(time order) 그리고 논리순(logical order) 방식에 따라 순서를 정한다. 의미의 일관성(coherence)과 통일성(unity)을 갖춘 완성된 단락(complete paragraph)을 작성한다. 문장은 1형식, 2형식, 3형식 그리고 5형식(tell동사의 용법)이다.

A	B
____ Ben wasn't at fault,	a. and the car behind him hit him.
____ He was stopping for a red light,	b. so the other driver got a ticket.
____ Yesterday, Ben had	c. to be more careful next time.
____ And the policeman told him	d. a car accident.

Rewriting

Listen to the paragraph. And dictate a paragraph you listened to using words and the phrases in the box.

Point

먼저 들려주는 지문을 주의깊게 듣는다. 그리고 박스 안에 주어진 단어를 이용하여 들었던 지문과 같은 지문을 작성한다. 지문을 들을 때는 먼저 의미가 파악되어야 하며, 박스 속에 주어진 단어를 연결하여 문장을 만들 때는 문장의 통일성(unity)에 유의한다. 특히 들을 때 잘 들리지 않는 관사, 조동사 will, 전치사 to와 in 등에 유의하여 문법적으로 바른 문장을 작성해야 한다. 또한 콤마(comma)와 물음표(question mark), 마침표(period), 그리고 대문자 (capital letter) 등 구두점(punctuation) 사용에 유의한다.

---

working/ office/ different/ few/ ago/ today/ secretaries/ computers/ key
data/ print/ copies/ when/ need/ easier/ be/ secretary/ now

Writing

Read to the paragraph. Then write the summary of the paragraph with the help of words and phrases in the boxes. (Summaries will vary.)

> **Point**
>
> 먼저 주어진 단락을 주의깊게 읽는다. 그리고 박스 안에 주어진 단어를 사용하여 읽었던 단락을 요약(summary)하여 요약문을 작성한다. 요약문은 3개의 문장으로 완성한다. 문장은 1형식과 2형식이다. 단락을 읽을 때는 먼저 의미가 파악되어야 하며, 박스 속에 주어진 단어를 연결하여 문장을 만들 때는 문장의 통일성(unity)에 유의해야 한다. 세련된 문장을 작성하기 위해서 공통 관계와 생략법 등을 최대한 활용하면서 문법을 바르게 적용해야 한다. 또한 콤마(comma)와 물음표(question mark), 마침표(period), 그리고 대문자(capital letter) 등 구두점(punctuation) 사용에 유의한다.

Jazz is a kind of music that began in the city of New Orleans, Louisiana, in the 1920s. It was very popular then, and still is today. Every night in New Orleans, jazz is played in many places around the city. Sometimes people wait in line just to hear it.

1	began/ New Orleans, Louisiana/ 1920s
2	it / as popular as/ then
3	sometimes/ in line/ hear

Summary: ....

....

....

Topic: ....

Main idea: ....

....

Match column A with column B to form sentences. Then rewrite a paragraph in order with the sentences.

Point

column A와 어울리는 표현을 column B에서 찾아 연결한 후 시간순(time order) 그리고 논리순(logical order) 방식에 따라 순서를 정한다. 의미의 일관성(coherence)과 통일성(unity)을 갖춘 완성된 단락(complete paragraph)을 작성한다. 문장은 1형식과 2형식 그리고 3형식이다.

A	B
____ I will visit him	a. to school in Los Angeles.
____ He went	b. is a doctor.
____ Now he lives	c. next winter.
____ My brother	d. in Orange County.

Rewriting

Listen to the paragraph. And dictate the paragraph you listened to using words and the phrases in the box.

Point

먼저 들려주는 지문을 주의깊게 듣는다. 그리고 박스 안에 주어진 단어를 이용하여 들었던 지문과 같은 지문을 작성한다. 지문을 들을 때는 먼저 의미가 파악되어야 하며, 박스 속에 주어진 단어를 연결하여 문장을 만들 때는 문장의 통일성(unity)에 유의한다. 특히 들을 때 잘 들리지 않는 관사, 조동사 will, 전치사 to와 in 등에 유의하여 문법적으로 바른 문장을 작성해야 한다. 또한 콤마(comma)와 물음표(question mark), 마침표(period), 그리고 대문자(capital letter) 등 구두점(punctuation) 사용에 유의한다. 문장은 3형식이다.

Sarah/ wanted/ drinkables/ vending machine
first/ got/ change
next/ put/ slot
after that/ pushed/ button/ under/ selection
then/ got/ drinkables

Writing

Read the paragraph. Then write the summary of the paragraph with the help of words and phrases in the boxes. (Summaries will vary.)

> **Point**
>
> 먼저 주어진 단락을 주의깊게 읽는다. 그리고 박스 안에 주어진 단어를 사용하여 읽었던 단락을 요약(summary)하여 요약문을 작성한다. 요약문은 3개의 문장으로 완성한다. 문장은 2형식과 3형식 그리고 5형식(make동사의 용법)이다. 단락을 읽을 때는 먼저 의미가 파악되어야 하며, 박스 속에 주어진 단어를 연결하여 문장을 만들 때는 문장의 통일성(unity)에 유의해야 한다. 세련된 문장을 작성하기 위해서 공통 관계와 생략법 등을 최대한 활용하면서 문법을 바르게 적용해야 한다. 또한 콤마(comma)와 물음표(question mark), 마침표(period), 그리고 대문자(capital letter) 등 구두점(punctuation) 사용에 유의한다.

Susan has an interesting job. She puts shoes on horses. Today, she drove to Mr. Green's house to put shoes on his horse, Silver. Silver was very nervous, but Susan talked to him quietly, so he became calm. She made his hooves smooth and nailed on the shoes. Susan really enjoys her work.

1	Susan/ puts/ horses
2	today/ shoes/ Mr. Green's/ Silver
3	nervous/ at first/ but/ made/ calm,/ before/ put/ horse

Summary:

Topic:

Main idea:

Read the paragraph; then choose a word for each number. Add the words to the paragraph and rewrite it on the lines below. (Answers will vary.)

Point

박스 안에 주어진 단어 중 적절한 단어를 번호에 맞게 선택한 후 주어진 문장에 추가하여 좀 더 길고 완벽한 문장을 만드는 학습이다. 이때 주의해야 할 사항은 의미의 일관성(coherence)이다. 먼저 박스 안에 주어진 단어의 의미가 파악되어야 한다. 문장은 전치사구를 동반한 1형식이며 to 부정사는 목적을 나타내고 있다.

The (1) man stopped at the (2) motel to sleep in a (3) room.

1. tall/ tired/ rich/ healthy
2. new/ old/ nice/ dreary
3. clean/ cold/ warm/ small

Rewriting

051

Rewrite the paragraph. Use capital letters, periods and apostrophes, if necessary.

Point

문장의 시작과 끝을 의미로 찾은 후 마침표(period)와 대문자(capital letter)를 활용하여 문장을 다시 구성한다. 그리고 아포스트로피(apostrophe)를 이용하여 문장을 완성한다. 대부분의 문장은 1형식과 3형식이다.

andy goes to class at 7:30 he listens to the teacher the teacher sometimes writes on the chalkboard andy looks at the chalkboard the teacher asks a question andy cant answer the question he must study his lesson

Rewriting

Make perfect sentences using the words in the box. (Answers will vary.)

> **Point**
>
> 박스 안에 주어진 단어를 이용하여 두 개의 문장을 만든다. 두 번째 문장의 주어는 첫 번째 문장의 주어에 유의하여 선택해야 하며 **not**의 선택은 두 번째 문장에서 상황에 맞게 고려해 본다. 뒤에 나오는 전치사구를 선택할 때는 문장 전체의 의미가 통할 수 있는 것을 선택한다. 문장은 3형식이다.

• Linda is drinking coffee. She is not drinking tea in her room.

Linda Eric I He She The family The boys My uncle His brother Her sister Your dog It They	am are is	(not)	watching eating drinking talking to listening to looking at reading studying coming buying opening sitting closing going selling sleeping	the windows the tapes their lessons her friend food their dinner TV coffee tea a book his lunch
eggs a newspaper dinner fruit his father her mother outside inside	in the kitchen. in your room. in the hospital. in his[her] room. at the dormitory. in their classroom. to the snack bar. to the gym. to the post office. to the library. to the police station. the garden.

Writing *ex* The boys are watching TV. They are not studying their lessons in your room.

1.

2.

3.

4.

5.

Match column A with column B to form sentences. Then rewrite a paragraph in order with the sentences.

Point

column A와 어울리는 표현을 column B에서 찾아 연결한 후 시간순(time order) 그리고 논리순(logical order) 방식에 따라 순서를 정한다. 의미의 일관성(coherence)과 통일성(unity)을 갖춘 완성된 단락(complete paragraph)을 작성한다. 문장은 1형식과 3형식이다.

A	B
____ I have	a. him tomorrow afternoon.
____ He lives in	b. needs some money.
____ I'll have to mail	c. New York.
____ My nephew	d. him the money.
____ I'll mail it to	e. to buy a money order.

Rewriting

Number the sentences in the correct time sequence. Then rewrite the sentences as a complete paragraph.

Point

시간순(time order) 방식과 논리순(logical order) 방식에 따라에 따라 순서에 맞게 번호를 적은 후 의미의 일관성(coherence)과 통일성(unity)을 갖춘 완성된 단락(complete paragraph)을 작성한다. 시간 표시의 접속사 then에 유의한다. 문장은 3형식과 4형식이다.

_____ He said, "May I see your driver's license?"
_____ A policeman stopped her.
_____ Then she said, "I don't have one."
_____ Anica was driving her car yesterday.
_____ He gave her a ticket.

Rewriting

Rewrite the paragraph with capital letters and periods, if necessary.

Point

문장의 시작과 끝을 의미로 찾은 후 마침표(period)와 대문자(capital letter)를 활용하여 문장을 다시 구성한다. 그리고 아포스트로피(apostrophe)를 이용하여 문장을 완성한다. 대부분의 문장은 부사구를 포함한 1형식과 3형식이다.

john gets up at 6:30 he takes a shower and shaves he puts on his clothes he goes to the cafeteria he sits down at the table and eats breakfast mark sits with john mark drinks a cup of coffee john doesnt drink a cup of coffee int the morning at 7:15 they walk to class

Rewriting

Read the paragraph; then choose a word for each number. Add the words to the paragraph and rewrite it on the lines below.(Answers will vary.)

Point

박스 안에 주어진 단어 중 적절한 단어를 번호에 맞게 선택한 후 주어진 문장에 추가하여 좀 더 길고 완벽한 문장을 만드는 학습이다. 이때 주의해야 할 사항은 의미의 일관성(coherence)이다. 먼저 박스 안에 주어진 단어의 의미가 파악되어야 한다. 문장은 전치사구를 동반한 1형식이며 to부정사는 목적을 나타내고 있다.

That (1) man didn't realize that he spilled coffee on the (2) carpet in his son's[daughter's] (3) house.

1. old/ young/ rude/ handsome
2. clean/ new/ dirty/ rugged
3. shabby/ new/ old/ beautiful

Rewriting

Combine the ideas into some sentences. And then rewrite a paragraph with the new sentences. (Rewritings will vary.)

Point

공통 관계(common relation)와 생략(ellipsis)법을 적용하여 문장을 간소화한다. 먼저 각각의 문장을 읽고 이해한 후 주어와 동사 그리고 목적어의 공통 관계를 파악한다. 그리고 생략법에 따라 문장을 결합시킨다. 무엇보다 문장의 통일성(unity)에 유의해야 한다. 필요한 경우에 적절한 접속사, 관계 대명사, 전치사, (대)명사, (대)동사, 조동사 그리고 형용사나 부사 등을 사용하여 단락 전체의 의미를 좀 더 명확하게 한다. 그러나 단락의 일관성(coherence)은 유지해야 한다. "/ /" 속에 포함된 문장들을 결합시켜 하나의 문장으로 다시 작성하여 단락을 완성한다. 문장은 3형식이다.

/ A computer has several parts with it. There is a keyboard. There is a monitor. There is a printer. // You use the keyboard to put the data into the computer. You use the printer to get the data out. /

Rewriting

Listen to the paragraph. And dictate the paragraph you listened to using words and the phrases in the box.

> **Point**
>
> 먼저 들려주는 지문을 주의깊게 듣는다. 그리고 박스 안에 주어진 단어를 0 용하여 들었던 지문과 같은 지문을 작성한다. 지문을 들을 때는 먼저 의미가 파악되어야 하며, 박스 속에 주어진 단어를 연결하여 문장을 만들 때는 문장의 통일성(unity)에 유의한다. 특히 들을 때 잘 들리지 않는 관사, 조동사 will, 전치사 to와 in 등에 유의하여 문법적으로 바른 문장을 작성해야 한다. 또한 콤마(comma)와 물음표(question mark), 마침표(period), 그리고 대문자(capital letter) 등 구두점(punctuation) 사용에 유의한다. 문장은 2형식과 3형식이다.

Tom/ likes/ travel/ on/ vacation/ last year/ able/ go/ London
while/ there/ able/ fly/ Ireland
rented/ car/ and/ able/ drive/ across/ east/ west
wasn't able/ get/ Paris/ but/ this year/ able/ Europe/ again

Writing

Read the paragraph below and change the simple future tense to future progressive. Rewrite the changed paragraph.

Point

단순미래시제(simple future tense)를 미래진행형(future progressive)으로 바꿔 각각의 문장을 다시 작성한다. 먼저 전환이 필요한 단어에 밑줄을 친 다음 시작한다. 또한 미래시제를 과거시제 그리고 현재시제 등으로 전환시켜 다양한 형태의 문장을 학습한다. 문장은 1형식과 3형식이다.

Larry will study for an important Korean test tomorrow morning. He will go to the library in the evening and stay there until ten o'clock. He will review his notes and will read the lessons in his book. His friend Ben will go with him and will give him a ride home.

Rewriting

Put these sentences in order. Then rewrite the sentences as one paragraph.

Point

시간순(time order) 방식과 논리순(logical order) 방식에 따라에 따라 순서에 맞게 번호를 적은 후 의미의 일관성(coherence)과 통일성(unity)을 갖춘 완성된 단락(complete paragraph)을 작성한다. 시간을 나타내는 부사 then과 first 등에 유의한다. 자동판매기(vendimg machine) 사용법을 참고로 해보자. 문장은 1형식, 3형식, 그리고 5형식(get동사의 용법)이다.

_____ First, put the money in the slot.
_____ Get it out.
_____ Then make your selection.
_____ How do you use this machine?
_____ Lift the door.
_____ Then wait until the snack drops.
_____ Push the button.

Rewriting

Match the phrases/clauses in column A with those in column B to form sentences. Then rewrite the sentences in order as one paragraph.

Point

column A와 어울리는 표현을 column B에서 찾아 연결한 후 시간순(time order) 그리고 논리순(logical order) 방식에 따라 순서를 정한다. 의미의 일관성(coherence)과 통일성(unity)을 갖춘 완성된 단락(complete paragraph)을 작성한다. 문장은 2형식과 3형식이다.

A	B
____ First, for my living room, ____ Then for my kitchen, ____ I got some new things ____ All these things were reasonable,	a. I bought a new oven and blender. b. I bought a new carpet and a coffee table. c. so now I enjoy my apartment more. d. for my apartment.

Rewriting

Read the paragraph. Then write the summary of the paragraph with the help of words and phrases in the boxes.(Summaries will vary.)

> **Point**
>
> 먼저 주어진 단락을 주의깊게 읽는다. 그리고 박스 안에 주어진 단어를 사용하여 읽었던 단락을 요약(summary)하여 요약문을 작성한다. 요약문은 3개의 문장으로 완성한다. 문장은 1형식과 2형식 그리고 3형식이다. 단락을 읽을 때는 먼저 의미가 파악되어야 하며, 박스 속에 주어진 단어를 연결하여 문장을 만들 때는 문장의 통일성(unity)에 유의해야 한다. 세련된 문장을 작성하기 위해서 공통 관계와 생략법 등을 최대한 활용하면서 문법을 바르게 적용해야 한다. 또한 콤마(comma)와 물음표(question mark), 마침표(period), 그리고 대문자(capital letter) 등 구두점(punctuation) 사용에 유의한다.

Eric is a diplomat. He is married and has two sons. He and his family have been to many places in the world. They all like to travel and enjoy living in different places and seeing new things. His sons like meeting children from other countries.

1	Eric/ diplomat
2	family/ travels/ around
3	enjoy/ and/ meeting

Summary:

Topic:

Main idea:

Listen to the paragraph. Write a title and then rewrite a similar paragraph using the words and the phrases in the boxes. (Rewritings will vary)

Point

먼저 들려주는 지문을 주의깊게 듣는다. 그리고 박스 안에 주어진 단어를 이용하여 들었던 지문과 유사한(similar) 지문과 제목(title)을 작성한다. 지문을 들을 때는 먼저 의미가 파악되어야 하며, 박스 속에 주어진 단어를 연결하여 문장을 만들 때는 문장의 통일성(unity)에 유의한다. 특히 들을 때 잘 들리지 않는 관사, 조동사 will, 전치사 to와 in 등에 유의하여 문법적으로 바른 문장을 작성해야 한다. 또한 콤마(comma)와 물음표(question mark), 마침표(period), 그리고 대문자(capital letter) 등 구두점(punctuation)의 사용에 유의한다. 문장은 1형식과 3형식이다.

1	people/ used/ wheels/ long time
2	earliest use/ 5,000 years ago/ Sumer
3	Assyrians/ 500 years later
4	people/ Europe/ more than 3,000 years ago

Title : ....

Rewriting

....

....

....

....

Make questions using the words in the box. (Answers will vary.)

> **Point**
>
> 의문사 What, Where, When 그리고 What time, How often 등을 이용한 의문문과 Do, Does를 이용한 의문문을 만든다. 어순(word order)에 유의해야 하며 동사(구)에 따른 목적어와 부사(구)가 의미와 부합해야 한다. 문장은 1형식과 3형식이다.

- What does Dustin study?
- How often do you see a movie?

Do Does What Where When What time How often	(do) (does)	you Dustin Mark Tony Ben Jane Fran Susan Wendy they	open read write eat do buy go study get up go to bed swim	every morning? every evening? every night? in class every morning? in the cafeteria every afternoon? a movie? lunch? English? breakfast? in the morning? in the afternoon? at night?

Writing   *ex* Does Tony eat every night?

1. _____

2. _____

3. _____

4. _____

5. _____

Part II

Intermediate Course

Make questions using the words in the box. (Answers will vary.)

> **Point**
> 의문대명사 Who를 주어로 하는 진행형 문장을 만든다. 동사(구)에 따른 목적어 혹은 부사구 선택에 유의하여 문장을 완성한다. 문장은 3형식이다.

• Who is going to the library?

| Who | are
is | eating
writing
coming
drinking
listening
watching
reading
going
talking | to the snack bar?
to the library?
a book in the park?
TV?
to the tapes?
orange juice?
to the office?
on the chalkboard?
breakfast?
to my father? |

Writing   *ex*   Who is watching TV?

1.

2.

3.

4.

5.

78 • Writing Bible

My father Eddy Beth Mr. Casey Ms. Watney Sam and Pat The teacher My kids	are is	eating writing coming drinking listening watching reading going talking	to the snack bar. to the library. a book in the park. TV. to the tapes. orange juice. to the office. on the chalkboard. breakfast. to my father.

Writing *ex* Sam and Pat are watching TV.

1.

2.

3.

4.

5.

Make sentences using words or phrases in the box. (Answers will vary.)

Point

빈도부사(frequency adverbs)를 활용한 문장을 만든다. 빈도부사는 주어와 일반동사 사이에 둔다. 또한 동사에 따른 부사(구) 혹은 목적어의 선택에 유의하여 문장을 완성한다. 문장은 1형식과 3 형식이다.

- I sometimes shave in the morning.

		take(s)	every night.
Bob		listen(s) to	on Wednesdays.
Jim		sleep(s)	after dinner.
George	never	come(s)	late.
I	hardly	hear(s)	to his[her] mother.
You	sometimes	watch(es)	the radio.
Jan	often	drink(s)	milk.
Anita	usually	shave(s)	in the classroom.
Helen	always	study(ies)	coffee.
The students		buy(s)	a plane.
The players		skate(s)	TV.
		play(s)	late.

Writing

ex I never drink coffee.

1.
2.
3.
4.
5.

Rewrite the paragraph. Put in capital letters, apostrophes, question marks and periods, if necessary.

Point

문장의 시작과 끝을 의미로 찾은 후 마침표(period)와 대문자(capital letter)를 활용하여 문장을 다시 구성한다. 그리고 콤마(comma), 아포스트로피(apostrophe) 그리고 물음표(question mark)를 이용하여 문장을 완성한다. 대부분의 문장은 1형식, 2형식 그리고 3형식이다.

larry took a trip to new york last month the weather wasnt very good it was cold and rainy larry didnt have his coat he was very upset what did larry do he bought a nice brown coat larry was in new york for one week it was a good trip

Rewriting

Number the sentences in the correct time sequence. Then rewrite the sentences as a complete paragraph.

Point

시간순(time order) 방식에 따라 순서에 맞게 번호를 적은후 의미의 일관성(coherence)과 통일성(unity)을 갖춘 완성된 단락(complete paragraph)을 작성한다. 시간 표시의 전치사와 접속사에 유의한다. 문장은 1형식, 2형식 그리고 3형식이다.

_____ After a short time, the waiter brought his food.
_____ He sat down and looked at the menu.
_____ At six o'clock, John was hungry.
_____ Then he ordered a big dinner.
_____ He went to a little restaurant near his house.

Rewriting

Match the phrases/clauses in column A with those in column B to form sentences. Then rewrite the sentences in order as dialog.

> **Point**
>
> column A와 어울리는 대화를 column B에서 찾아 일관성을 갖춘 대화문(dialog)을 완성한다. 의미의 일관성(coherence)과 통일성(unity)을 갖춘 완성된 대화문(complete dialog)을 작성한다. 문장은 1형식, 2형식 그리고 3형식이다.

A	B
____ I've already checked there. Where else could he be?	a. He could be in the dormitory. I saw him there a few minutes ago.
____ Thanks. I'll try the city library.	b. I'm not sure. He uses both.
____ Where is Meg?	c. Good luck!
____ Which one? The city or school library?	d. Well, then he may be at the library. He has a test tomorrow.

Rewriting

A :

B :

A :

B :

A :

B :

A :

B :

Read the paragraph; then choose a word for each number. Add the words to the paragraph and rewrite it on the lines below. (Answers will vary.)

Point

박스 안에 주어진 단어 중 적절한 단어를 번호에 맞게 선택한 후 주어진 문장에 추가하여 좀 더 길고 완벽한 문장을 만드는 학습이다. 이때 주의해야 할 사항은 의미의 일관성(coherence)이다. 먼저 박스 안에 주어진 단어의 의미가 파악되어야 한다. 문장은 2형식과 3형식이다.

Susan is a (1) girl because she made a (2) score on her test. Now she can (3) her weekend. She knows she will (4).

1. dull/ nice/ happy/ healthy
2. high/ strong/ low/ weak
3. finish/ enjoy/ study/ waste
4. graduate/ stay longer

Rewriting

Read the paragraph. Then write the summary of the paragraph with the help of words and phrases in the box. (Summaries will vary.)

> **Point**
>
> 먼저 주어진 단락을 주의깊게 읽는다. 그리고 박스 안에 주어진 단어를 사용하여 읽었던 단락을 요약(summary)하여 요약문을 작성한다. 요약문은 1개의 문장으로 완성한다. 문장은 2형식이다. 단락을 읽을 때는 먼저 의미가 파악되어야 하며, 박스 속에 주어진 단어를 연결하여 문장을 만들 때는 문장의 통일성(unity)에 유의해야 한다. 세련된 문장을 작성하기 위해서 공통 관계와 생략법 등을 최대한 활용하면서 문법을 바르게 적용해야 한다. 또한 콤마(comma)와 물음표(question mark), 마침표(period), 그리고 대문자(capital letter) 등 구두점(punctuation) 사용에 유의한다.

A dictionary will give you a lot of information. It will tell you how to spell a word, how to say it, and how to use it. Sometimes one word can mean different things; a dictionary will explain them and give examples. People who want to speak, read and write well should have a good dictionary and use it often.

| information/ good dictionary/ is important/ who/ use language |

Summary:

Topic:

Main idea:

Listen to the paragraph. And dictate a paragraph you listened to using words and the phrases in the box.

Point

먼저 들려주는 지문을 주의깊게 듣는다. 그리고 박스 안에 주어진 단어를 이용하여 들었던 지문과 같은 지문을 작성한다. 지문을 들을 때는 먼저 의미가 파악되어야 하며, 박스 속에 주어진 단어를 연결하여 문장을 만들 때는 문장의 통일성(unity)에 유의한다. 특히 들을 때 잘 들리지 않는 관사, 조동사 will, 전치사 to와 in 등에 유의하여 문법적으로 바른 문장을 작성해야 한다. 또한 콤마(comma)와 물음표(question mark), 마침표(period), 그리고 대문자(capital letter) 등 구두점(punctuation) 사용에 유의한다. 문장은 1형식과 3형식이다.

Mark/ find/ car keys/ morning
looked/ everywhere/ apartment
then/ realized/ left/ car/ locked/ doors
tried/ open/ coat hanger/ but/ work
didn't/ time/ get/ new key/ rode/ office

Writing

Read the paragraph. Then write the summary of the paragraph with the help of words and phrases in the box. (Summaries will vary.)

> **Point**
>
> 먼저 주어진 단락을 주의깊게 읽는다. 그리고 박스 안에 주어진 단어를 사용하여 읽었던 단락을 요약(summary) 하여 요약문을 작성한다. 요약문은 1개의 문장으로 완성한다. 문장은 3형식이다. 단락을 읽을 때는 먼저 의미가 파악되어야 하며, 박스 속에 주어진 단어를 연결하여 문장을 만들 때는 문장의 통일성(unity)에 유의해야 한다. 세련된 문장을 작성하기 위해서 공통 관계와 생략법 등을 최대한 활용하면서 문법을 바르게 적용해야 한다. 또한 콤마(comma)와 물음표(question mark), 마침표(period), 그리고 대문자(capital letter) 등 구두점 (punctuation) 사용에 유의한다.

Do you usually spend too much money at the grocery store? Here are two things that may help. First, eat a good meal before you go. Don't shop for food when you're hungry, or you'll get more than you need. Also, plan your meals for the week ahead. Write everything that's necessary for those meals on a piece of paper, and don't buy anything else.

---

save/ by/ eating/ planning/ meals/ before/ grocery store

Summary:

Topic:

Main idea:

Make questions using the words in the box. (Answers will vary.)

Point

'How many+명사'를 활용한 의문문을 만든다. 이때 명사는 셀 수 있는 복수명사(countable nouns)가 되어야 하며 동사에 대한 목적어가 된다. 그러나 be동사가 사용되면 명사는 주어가 된다. 전체적으로 뒤에 나오는 부사(구)와 의미상 일치가 되도록 문장을 완성한다. 문장은 1형식과 3형식이다.

- How many months are there in a year? — 1형식
- How many friends do you have? — 3형식

| How many | students
teachers
women
men
notebooks
chalkboards
words
months
seconds
friends
meals | do
does
are | you
he
she
they
there | have
see
learn
buy | in the classroom?
on the desk?
every day?
every night?
in a day?
in a year?
in a minute? |

Writing   *ex*   How many seconds are there in a day?

1.
2.
3.
4.
5.

Make sentences using words or phrases in the box. (Answers will vary.)

> **Point**
>
> '주어+want+to 부정사'의 구문을 만든다. 수(단수, 복수)에 따른 동사의 일치에 유의해야 하며 to 부정사의 목적어를 선택할 때 의미상 적절성에 유의하며 문장을 완성한다. don't와 doesn't는 선택이다. 문장은 3형식이다.

- Nick wants to play a golf.
- Sarah doesn't want to study that lesson.

Larry Nick Mike Greg Rosa Judy Ann Sarah Scott and Liz Rick and Cindy	(don't) (doesn't)	want(s) to	study go (to) speak have read write learn do look at play drink shave buy	a golf. the picture. that lesson. Korea. Korean. the library. abroad for study. coffee. chicken. for lunch. a novel. in the morning.

Writing   *ex* Sarah wants to learn Korean.

1.
2.
3.
4.
5.

Read the paragraph. Then write the summary of the paragraph with the help of words and phrases in the boxes. (Summaries will vary.)

> **Point**
>
> 먼저 주어진 단락을 주의깊게 읽는다. 그리고 박스 안에 주어진 단어를 사용하여 읽었던 단락을 요약(summary)하여 요약문을 작성한다. 요약문은 2개의 문장으로 완성한다. 문장은 3형식과 5형식(keep동사의 용법)이다. 단락을 읽을 때는 먼저 의미가 파악되어야 하며, 박스 속에 주어진 단어를 연결하여 문장을 만들 때는 문장의 통일성(unity)에 유의해야 한다. 세련된 문장을 작성하기 위해서 공통 관계와 생략법 등을 최대한 활용하면서 문법을 바르게 적용해야 한다. 또한 콤마(comma)와 물음표(question mark), 마침표(period), 그리고 대문자(capital letter) 등 구두점(punctuation) 사용에 유의한다.

When Andy has some spare time, he works in his yard. Every day he picks up the leaves and once a week he cuts the grass. Last week he put flowers around the trees and in front of the house. Next fall he's going to put some vegetables in his back yard. Andy's yard really keeps him busy.

1	spend/ time/ working/ yard
2	it/ keeps/ busy

Summary:

Topic:

Main idea:

Read the paragraph. Then write the summary of the paragraph with the help of words and phrases in the boxes. (Summaries will vary.)

Point

먼저 주어진 단락을 주의깊게 읽는다. 그리고 박스 안에 주어진 단어를 사용하여 읽었던 단락을 요약(summary)하여 요약문을 작성한다. 요약문은 2개의 문장으로 완성한다. 문장은 2형식과 3형식이다. 단락을 읽을 때는 먼저 의미가 파악되어야 하며, 박스 속에 주어진 단어를 연결하여 문장을 만들 때는 문장의 통일성(unity)에 유의해야 한다. 세련된 문장을 작성하기 위해서 공통 관계와 생략법 등을 최대한 활용하면서 문법을 바르게 적용해야 한다. 또한 콤마(comma)와 물음표(question mark), 마침표(period), 그리고 대문자(capital letter) 등 구두점(punctuation) 사용에 유의한다.

When Mary went outside this morning to check the weather, the sky was clear. She decided to walk to work. She left her umbrella at home because she didn't think she needed it. About 5:00 p.m. the weather started to change. Soon there were big, black clouds in the sky. It began to rain while she was walking home, and her clothes got very wet.

1	Mary/ take/ umbrella/ work
2	started/ while/ walking/ and/ wet

Summary: ....

....

....

....

Topic: ....

Main idea: ....

....

78

Rewrite the paragraph. Put in capital letters, apostrophes, commas, quotation marks, question marks and periods, if necessary.

Point

문장의 시작과 끝을 의미로 찾은 후 마침표(period)와 대문자(capital letter)를 활용하여 문장을 다시 구성한다. 그리고 아포스트로피(apostrophe), 물음표(question mark), 따옴표(quotation mark) 그리고 콤마(comma)를 이용하여 문장을 완성한다. 대부분의 문장은 1형식과 3형식이다.

yesterday a teacher phoned from my sons school he said your son hurt his leg can you come to the school right now ill be there in a few minutes i said i left the house ran to my car and drove to the school i got there in fifteen minutes

Rewriting

Number the sentences in the correct time sequence. Then rewrite the sentences as a complete paragraph.

Point

시간순(time order) 방식과 논리순(logical order) 방식에 따라에 따라 순서에 맞게 번호를 적은 후 의미의 일관성(coherence)과 통일성(unity)을 갖춘 완성된 단락(complete paragraph)을 작성한다. 시간 표시의 접속사 then과 장소 표시의 전치사 from에 유의한다. 문장은 1형식과 3형식이다.

_____ From the bank, she took a bus downtown.
_____ She counted her money. She didn't have much.
_____ Then she walked to the bank.
_____ Angela needed to buy a few things.
_____ She cashed a check there and got some money.

Rewriting

Match the phrases/ clauses in column A with those in column B to form sentences. Then rewrite the sentences in order as one paragraph.

Point

column A와 어울리는 표현을 column B에서 찾아 연결한 후 시간순(time order) 그리고 논리순(logical order) 방식에 따라 순서를 정한다. 의미의 일관성(coherence)과 통일성(unity)을 갖춘 완성된 단락(complete paragraph)을 작성한다. 문장은 1형식과 2형식 그리고 3형식이다.

A	B
____ Lorena and Kim	a. the rooms every day.
____ They clean	b. the sheets, blankets and pillows.
____ First, they wash	c. so they like it.
____ Then they change	d. work in a hotel.
____ Their work is not so hard,	e. the bathrooms.

Rewriting

081

Read the paragraph; then choose a word for each number. Add the words to the paragraph and rewrite it on the lines below. (Answers will vary.)

Point

박스 안에 주어진 단어 중 적절한 단어를 번호에 맞게 선택한 후 주어진 문장에 추가하여 좀 더 길고 완벽한 문장을 만드는 학습이다. 이때 주의해야 할 사항은 의미의 일관성(coherence)이다. 먼저 박스 안에 주어진 단어의 의미가 파악되어야 한다. 문장은 1형식, 2형식 그리고 3형식이다.

Howard and Helen went to a(n) (1) restaurant. The food was (2). The service was (3). They were both (4) and decided to (5).

1. new/ old/ noisy
2. tasty/ salty/ greasy
3. good/ bad/ slow
4. unhappy/ satisfied/ hungry
5. leave/ come again/ return

Rewriting

Read the paragraph. Then write the summary of the paragraph with the help of words and phrases in the boxes. (Summaries will vary.)

> **Point**
>
> 먼저 주어진 단락을 주의깊게 읽는다. 그리고 박스 안에 주어진 단어를 사용하여 읽었던 단락을 요약(summary)하여 요약문을 작성한다. 요약문은 2개의 문장으로 완성한다. 문장은 1형식과 2형식이다. 단락을 읽을 때는 먼저 의미가 파악되어야 하며, 박스 속에 주어진 단어를 연결하여 문장을 만들 때는 문장의 통일성(unity)에 유의해야 한다. 세련된 문장을 작성하기 위해서 공통 관계와 생략법 등을 최대한 활용하면서 문법을 바르게 적용해야 한다. 또한 콤마(comma)와 물음표(question mark), 마침표(period), 그리고 대문자(capital letter) 등 구두점(punctuation) 사용에 유의한다.

It had been a long day for Carl. He had begun work early and had worked hard. He'd only taken 10 minutes to eat a sandwich at lunch. He was tired and ready to go home. The phone rang just as he was opening the door to leave. He closed the door behind him and left.

1	Carl/ tired/ long/ day/ work
2	rang/ as/ leaving/ but/ too/ to answer

Summary:

Topic:

Main idea:

Make questions using the words in the box. (Answers will vary.)

Point

'의문사+be동사(과거형)+주어'의 구문을 장소와 시간을 나타내는 부사(구)와 결합시켜 하나의 완전한 문장을 완성한다. 여기에서 be동사의 의미는 '있다(존재)'의 뜻으로 쓰인다. 문장은 1형식이다.

- Who was in the lab this morning?
- Where were the children last night?

Who What Where When	was wasn't were weren't	Jim and Tina Arthur Max Alex Paula Cathy Janet the dictionary the children You	in the lab(?) in Canada(?) in class(?) in the box(?) in England(?) in the room on the bulletin board on the chair on the table at the restaurant	in 1988? last month? last year? five years ago? yesterday? last night? last week? at 9:00 p.m.? two weeks ago?

Writing

ex Where was Alex at 9:00 p.m.?

1.
2.
3.
4.
5.

Rewrite the paragraph with capital letters, apostrophes and periods, if necessary.

Point

문장의 시작과 끝을 의미로 찾은 후 마침표(period)와 대문자(capital letter)를 활용하여 문장을 다시 구성한다. 마지막으로 아포스트로피(apostrophe)를 이용하여 문장을 완성한다. 대부분의 문장은 1형식, 2형식 그리고 3형식이다.

tim hurt his right knee last week he saw the doctor and he took his medicine tim didnt come to class for two days he went to the doctors office again the doctor looked at his knee and put medicine on it the next day his knee was all right

Rewriting

Match the phrases/clauses in column A with those in column B to form sentences. Then rewrite the sentences in order as one paragraph.

> **Point**
>
> column A와 어울리는 표현을 column B에서 찾아 연결한 후 시간순(time order) 그리고 논리순(logical order) 방식에 따라 순서를 정한다. 의미의 일관성(coherence)과 통일성(unity)을 갖춘 완성된 단락(complete paragraph)을 작성한다. 문장은 1형식, 2형식 그리고 3형식이다.

A	B
____ The work day in Seoul ____ Most of the people drive ____ They get dressed and ____ Most people get up ____ There are some people who live so far,	a. eat breakfast then they start for work. b. their cars to work, but some take the bus or subway. c. between 5:30 and 6:00. d. starts between 7:00 and 9:00. e. they have to take a train.

> **Rewriting**

_____

_____

_____

_____

_____

Read the paragraph; then choose a word for each number. Add the words to the paragraph and rewrite it on the lines below. (Answers will vary.)

Point

박스 안에 주어진 단어 중 적절한 단어를 번호에 맞게 선택한 후 주어진 문장에 추가하여 좀 더 길고 완벽한 문장을 만드는 학습이다. 이때 주의해야 할 사항은 의미의 일관성(coherence)이다. 먼저 박스 안에 주어진 단어의 의미가 파악되어야 한다. 문장은 3형식이다.

Ben had to (1). He had the (2), but he didn't have (3). He had to go to (4) for it. When he got there he had to (5).

1. change tires/ deposit some money/ mail a package
2. address/ tools/ cash
3. a deposit slip/ a stamp/ a spare tire
4. the post office/ a tire store/ the bank
5. stand in line/ go back home/ pay a lot

Rewriting

087

Combine the ideas into some sentences. And then rewrite a paragraph with the new sentences. (Rewritings will vary.)

Point

공통 관계(common relation)와 생략(ellipsis)법을 적용하여 문장을 간소화한다. 먼저 각각의 문장을 읽고 이해한 후 주어와 동사 그리고 목적어의 공통 관계를 파악한다. 그리고 생략법에 따라 문장을 결합시킨다. 무엇보다 문장의 통일성(unity)에 유의해야 한다. 필요한 경우에 적절한 접속사, 관계 대명사, 전치사, (대)명사, (대)동사, 조동사 그리고 형용사나 부사 등을 사용하여 단락 전체의 의미를 좀 더 명확하게 한다. 그러나 단락의 일관성(coherence)은 유지해야 한다. "/ /" 속에 포함된 문장들을 결합시켜 하나의 문장으로 다시 작성하여 단락을 완성한다. 문장은 3형식과 4형식(tell동사의 용법)이다.

/ What causes sleep? Can anyone tell you? // We know that all people need sleep. All animals also need sleep. // Plants may also need sleep. Some people think so. // What causes sleep? Not many people can say. But all of us need it. /

Rewriting

Listen to the paragraph. And dictate a paragraph you listened to using words and the phrases in the box.

Point

먼저 들려주는 지문을 주의깊게 듣는다. 그리고 박스 안에 주어진 단어를 이용하여 들었던 지문과 같은 지문을 작성한다. 지문을 들을 때는 먼저 의미가 파악되어야 하며, 박스 속에 주어진 단어를 연결하여 문장을 만들 때는 문장의 통일성(unity)에 유의한다. 특히 들을 때 잘 들리지 않는 관사, 조동사 will, 전치사 to와 in 등에 유의하여 문법적으로 바른 문장을 작성해야 한다. 또한 콤마(comma)와 물음표(question mark), 마침표(period), 그리고 대문자(capital letter) 등 구두점(punctuation) 사용에 유의한다. 문장은 1형식, 2형식 그리고 3형식이다.

lunch/ restaurants/ served/ three
first/ salad/ coffee next/ meat/ vegetables/ plate
rolls/ kind of/ served/ meal
dessert/ last/ have to/ extra

Writing

Read the paragraph. Then write the summary of the paragraph with the help of words and phrases in the boxes. (Summaries will vary.)

> **Point**
>
> 먼저 주어진 단락을 주의깊게 읽는다. 그리고 박스 안에 주어진 단어를 사용하여 읽었던 단락을 요약(summary)하여 요약문을 작성한다. 요약문은 2개의 문장으로 완성한다. 문장은 3형식이다. 단락을 읽을 때는 먼저 의미가 파악되어야 하며, 박스 속에 주어진 단어를 연결하여 문장을 만들 때는 문장의 통일성(unity)에 유의해야 한다. 세련된 문장을 작성하기 위해서 공통 관계와 생략법 등을 최대한 활용하면서 문법을 바르게 적용해야 한다. 또한 콤마(comma)와 물음표(question mark), 마침표(period), 그리고 대문자(capital letter) 등 구두점(punctuation) 사용에 유의한다.

Yesterday after school, George and his friends played baseball in the playing ground near his house. At six o'clock, George's mother told him that dinner was ready, but he didn't want to come inside. After waiting for half an hour, the family decided to eat dinner without him. George came home when it got dark, but everyone had finished eating by that time.

1	George/ missed/ yesterday
2	playing/ and/ not/ inside/ when/ ready

Summary:

Topic:

Main idea:

PART II • 103

Make perfect sentences using the words in the box. (Answers will vary.)

Point

수량 표시의 형용사구를 활용하여 다양한 표현을 만든다. 동사와 목적어의 관계, 그리고 동사와 부사구(전치사구)의 관계를 고려하여 완벽한 문장을 만든다. 또한 'There is[are] ~' 구문을 놓쳐서는 안 되며 부사구는 선택적이다. 문장은 1형식(There 구문)과 3형식이다.

- Joe bought 2 cans of corn at the store.
- Ann sold 5 bars of soap at the drugstore.

Joe	ate	8 ounces of	milk		the drugstore.
Nick	got	1 tube of	tomato		the bathroom.
Steve	are	2 cans of	pie		the sandwich.
Patty	bought	3 bottles of	pepper	at	the restaurant.
Ann	sold	1 bowl of	ice cream	in	the table.
Cindy	is	1 quart of	toothpaste	on	lunch.
There	put	5 bars of	soap	for	the container.
They	needed	3 pieces of	juice		breakfast.
		4 gallons of	egg		the store.
			salt		the bottle.

Writing

ex Cindy bought 3 pieces of soap for the bathroom.

1.
2.
3.
4.
5.

Read the paragraph. Then write the summary of the paragraph with the help of words and phrases in the boxes. (Summaries will vary.)

> **Point**
>
> 먼저 주어진 단락을 주의깊게 읽는다. 그리고 박스 안에 주어진 단어를 사용하여 읽었던 단락을 요약(summary)하여 요약문을 작성한다. 요약문은 2개의 문장으로 완성한다. 문장은 3형식과 5형식(make동사의 용법)이다. 단락을 읽을 때는 먼저 의미가 파악되어야 하며, 박스 속에 주어진 단어를 연결하여 문장을 만들 때는 문장의 통일성(unity)에 유의해야 한다. 세련된 문장을 작성하기 위해서 공통 관계와 생략법 등을 최대한 활용하면서 문법을 바르게 적용해야 한다. 또한 콤마(comma)와 물음표(question mark), 마침표(period), 그리고 대문자(capital letter) 등 구두점(punctuation) 사용에 유의한다.

During the last part of the 1800's, people in the United States and Switzerland made machines that could make clocks. These machines made clocks faster and cheaper than men could. They made many different kinds of clocks. Some were alarm clocks. Others told the day, month, and year as well as the time.

1	late 1800's/ people/ U.S./ Switzerland/ that/ kinds/ clocks
2	machines/ faster/ cheaper/ than/ could

Summary:

Topic:

Main idea:

Rewrite the paragraph. Use capital letters, commas, periods and apostrophes, if necessary.

Point

문장의 시작과 끝을 의미로 찾은 후 마침표(period)와 대문자(capital letter)를 활용하여 문장을 다시 구성한다. 그리고 열거를 나타내는 콤마(comma)와 아포스트로피(apostrophe)를 이용하여 문장을 완성한다. 대부분의 문장은 1형식, 2형식 그리고 3형식이다.

mike loves to cook he cooks all kinds of dishes but his favorite dishes are desserts he says cooking is very relaxing when he is working in the kitchen he thinks only about cooking he doesnt think about work or bad thing he can bake big and beautiful cakes with fruit or with chocolate

Rewriting

Read the paragraph. Then change present tense to past tense. Underline the words that need to be changed. Rewrite the changed paragraph.

Point

현재시제(present tense)를 과거시제(past tense)로 바꿔 각각의 문장을 다시 작성한다. 먼저 전환이 필요한 단어에 밑줄을 긋는다. 가능한 경우 미래시제(future tense)로 바꾸어 학습한다. 문장은 1형식, 2형식 그리고 3형식이다.

> The Lucky Department has a big sale today. They have a lot of good deals. In the variety store, they have plastic dishes and glass items for much less than usual. Silk skirts are 20% off, and cotton clothes are 45% off. The discount on the jewelry is the best. Gold rings, gold chains, silver bracelets and copper earrings sell for 50% off.

Rewriting

Number the sentences in the correct time sequence. Then rewrite the sentences as a complete paragraph.

Point

시간순(time order) 방식에 따라 순서에 맞게 번호를 적은 후 의미의 일관성(coherence)과 통일성(unity)을 갖춘 완성된 단락(complete paragraph)을 작성한다. 시간 표시의 부사 first와 접속사 then에 유의해야 한다. 문장은 2형식, 3형식 그리고 4형식이다.

_____ She didn't want it because it was too small.
_____ She put a deposit on it.
_____ Karen wanted to rent a new apartment.
_____ Then she looked at a two-bedroom apartment.
_____ First, the manager showed her a one-bedroom apartment.

Rewriting

Match the phrases/clauses in column A with those in column B to form sentences. Then rewrite the sentences in order as one paragraph.

Point

column A와 어울리는 표현을 column B에서 찾아 연결한 후 시간순(time order) 그리고 논리순(logical order) 방식에 따라 순서를 정한다. 의미의 일관성(coherence)과 통일성(unity)을 갖춘 완성된 단락(complete paragraph)을 작성한다. 문장은 1형식과 3형식이다.

A	B
____ Mark and Sara took ____ Mark and Sara both ____ They took a long trip ____ They went sightseeing every day and ____ They used many	a. and stayed overnight in many nice hotels. b. a vacation. c. enjoyed their trip. d. rolls of film. e. took a lot of pictures of mountains and lakes.

Rewriting

Read the paragraph; then choose a word for each number. Add the words to the paragraph and rewrite it on the lines below. (Answers will vary.)

Point

박스 안에 주어진 단어 중 적절한 단어를 번호에 맞게 선택한 후 주어진 문장에 추가하여 좀 더 길고 완벽한 문장을 만드는 학습이다. 이때 주의해야 할 사항은 의미의 일관성(coherence)이다. 먼저 박스 안에 주어진 단어의 의미가 파악되어야 한다. 문장은 전치사구를 포함한 3형식이다.

The (1) man bought a(n) (2) book from the (3) clerk in the bookstore. He took it home and read it (4). He thought it was a very (5) book.

1. tall/ intelligent/ foolish/ tough
2. new/ old/ medical/ expensive
3. old/ young/ nice/ kind
4. slowly/ carefully/ quietly/ fast
5. interesting/ boring/ exciting/ special

Rewriting

Combine the ideas into some sentences. And then rewrite a paragraph with the new sentences. (Rewritings will vary.)

Point

공통 관계(common relation)와 생략(ellipsis)법을 적용하여 문장을 간소화한다. 먼저 각각의 문장을 읽고 이해한 후 주어와 동사 그리고 목적어의 공통 관계를 파악한다. 그리고 생략법에 따라 문장을 결합한다. 무엇보다 문장의 통일성(unity)에 유의해야 한다. 필요한 경우에 적절한 접속사, 관계 대명사, 전치사, (대)명사, (대)동사, 조동사 그리고 형용사나 부사 등을 사용하여 단락 전체의 의미를 좀 더 명확하게 한다. 그러나 단락의 일관성(coherence)은 유지해야 한다. "/ /" 속에 포함된 문장들을 결합시켜 하나의 문장으로 다시 작성하여 단락을 완성한다. 문장은 2형식과 3형식이다.

/ Chris is an automobile mechanic. He can fix the air conditioner in a car. He can replace the battery in a car. He can fix or replace the radiator in a car. He can repair any problems with a car. // He can figure out any problems with a car. He used to work for a car company. His job was to assemble cars. /

Rewriting

Listen to the paragraph. And dictate a paragraph you listened to using words and the phrases in the box.

Point

먼저 들려주는 지문을 주의깊게 듣는다. 그리고 박스 안에 주어진 단어를 이용하여 들었던 지문과 같은 지문을 작성한다. 지문을 들을 때는 먼저 의미가 파악되어야 하며, 박스 속에 주어진 단어를 연결하여 문장을 만들 때는 문장의 통일성(unity)에 유의한다. 특히 들을 때 잘 들리지 않는 관사, 조동사 will, 전치사 to와 in 등에 유의하여 문법적으로 바른 문장을 작성해야 한다. 또한 콤마(comma)와 물음표(question mark), 마침표(period), 그리고 대문자(capital letter) 등 구두점(punctuation) 사용에 유의한다. 문장은 1형식과 2형식이다.

---

aluminum/ electrical/ conductor
used/ production/ circuits/ wires
as good as/ silver/ conducting/ a lot/ cheaper
besides/ beautiful/ use/ ugly/ covered/ insulation
silver/ jewelry/ better/ electrical

Writing

Read to the paragraph. Then write the summary of the paragraph with the help of words and phrases in the boxes. (Summaries will vary.)

> **Point**
>
> 먼저 주어진 단락을 주의깊게 읽는다. 그리고 박스 안에 주어진 단어를 사용하여 읽었던 단락을 요약(summary)하여 요약문을 작성한다. 요약문은 2개의 문장으로 완성한다. 문장은 1형식과 3형식이다. 단락을 읽을 때는 먼저 의미가 파악되어야 하며, 박스 속에 주어진 단어를 연결하여 문장을 만들 때는 문장의 통일성(unity)에 유의해야 한다. 세련된 문장을 작성하기 위해서 공통 관계와 생략법 등을 최대한 활용하면서 문법을 바르게 적용해야 한다. 또한 콤마(comma)와 물음표(question mark), 마침표(period), 그리고 대문자(capital letter) 등 구두점(punctuation) 사용에 유의한다.

Paula just got back from her vacation. Now she's sitting in class and thinking about Florida, the ocean and the sun. Her teacher thinks that she's reading her lesson, but she's not. Her book is open, but her mind isn't on the words on the page. She's really thinking about her trip. That's much more interesting to her than her textbook.

1	Paula/ class/ but/ not/ textbook
2	thinking/ vacation/ Florida

Summary:

Topic:

Main idea:

1oo

Read the paragraph; then choose a word for each number. Add the words to the paragraph and rewrite it on the lines below. (Answers will vary.)

> **Point**
>
> 박스 안에 주어진 단어 중 적절한 단어를 번호에 맞게 선택한 후 주어진 문장에 추가하여 좀 더 길고 완벽한 문장을 만드는 학습이다. 이때 주의해야 할 사항은 의미의 일관성(coherence)이다. 먼저 박스 안에 주어진 단어의 의미가 파악되어야 한다. 문장은 1형식, 2형식 그리고 3형식이다.

Max owns (1). He works very hard. He has to (2). His (3) helps him. The work is (4). He makes (5) money. He and his family are happy because the (6) is theirs.

1. a gas station/ a motel/ a cafeteria
2. clean up the rooms/ cook the food/ repair cars
3. son/ brother/ daughter
4. easy/ difficult/ interesting
5. a lot of/ a little/ enough
6. gas station/ motel/ cafeteria

Rewriting

1o1

Listen to the paragraph. And dictate a paragraph you listened to using words and the phrases in the box.

Point

먼저 들려주는 지문을 주의깊게 듣는다. 그리고 박스 안에 주어진 단어를 이용하여 들었던 지문과 같은 지문을 작성한다. 지문을 들을 때는 먼저 의미가 파악되어야 하며, 박스 속에 주어진 단어를 연결하여 문장을 만들 때는 문장의 통일성(unity)에 유의한다. 특히 들을 때 잘 들리지 않는 관사, 조동사 will, 전치사 to와 in 등에 유의하여 문법적으로 바른 문장을 작성해야 한다. 또한 콤마(comma)와 물음표(question mark), 마침표(period), 그리고 대문자(capital letter) 등 구두점(punctuation) 사용에 유의한다. 문장은 3형식이다.

> computers/ can/ things/ these days
> first of all/ add/ numbers/ also/ print/ fast and well
> you/ letters/ people/ all over the world
> information/ school/ business
> also/ shop/ on the computer/ movie

Writing

Listen to the paragraph. Write a title, and then rewrite a similar paragraph using the words and the phrases in the boxes. (Answers will vary.)

Point

먼저 들려주는 지문을 주의깊게 듣는다. 그리고 박스 안에 주어진 단어를 이용하여 들었던 지문과 유사한(similar) 지문과 제목(title)을 작성한다. 지문을 들을 때는 먼저 의미가 파악되어야 하며, 박스 속에 주어진 단어를 연결하여 문장을 만들 때는 문장의 통일성(unity)에 유의한다. 특히 들을 때 잘 들리지 않는 관사, 조동사 will, 전치사 to와 in 등에 유의하여 문법적으로 바른 문장을 작성해야 한다. 또한 콤마(comma)와 물음표(question mark), 마침표(period), 그리고 대문자(capital letter) 등 구두점(punctuation) 사용에 유의한다. 문장은 1형식과 3형식이다.

1	skunk/ sleeps/ the day/ looks/ food/ night
2	eats/ animals/ birds/ eggs/ fruit
3	favorite meal/ bugs
4	can't see/ but/ good ears/ nose/ helps/ find food/ stay safe

Title : _____

Rewriting

_____

_____

_____

_____

103

Read the paragraph. Then write the summary of the paragraph with the help of words and phrases in the boxes. (Summaries will vary.)

> **Point**
>
> 먼저 주어진 단락을 주의깊게 읽는다. 그리고 박스 안에 주어진 단어를 사용하여 읽었던 단락을 요약(summary)하여 요약문을 작성한다. 요약문은 3개의 문장으로 완성한다. 문장은 1형식과 3형식이다. 단락을 읽을 때는 먼저 의미가 파악되어야 하며, 박스 속에 주어진 단어를 연결하여 문장을 만들 때는 문장의 통일성(unity)에 유의해야 한다. 세련된 문장을 작성하기 위해서 공통 관계와 생략법 등을 최대한 활용하면서 문법을 바르게 적용해야 한다. 또한 콤마(comma)와 물음표(question mark), 마침표(period), 그리고 대문자(capital letter) 등 구두점(punctuation) 사용에 유의한다.

Sally works in a large and busy office in a big city. She doesn't get much exercise at her job, so when she goes home from work, she likes to run. She tries to run four miles every day. She likes to run on roads in the country because it's very quiet and calm there. She can listen to the birds and look at the trees and flowers. She always feels relaxed after she runs.

1	Sally/ doesn't/ exercise/ her job/ so/ run/ country/ after
2	enjoys/ there
3	always/ relaxed/ after

Summary:

Topic:

Main idea:

Read the paragraph; then choose a word for each number. Add the words to the paragraph and rewrite it on the lines below. (Answers will vary.)

Point

박스 안에 주어진 단어 중 적절한 단어를 번호에 맞게 선택한 후 주어진 문장에 추가하여 좀 더 길고 완벽한 문장을 만드는 학습이다. 이때 주의해야 할 사항은 의미의 일관성(coherence)이다. 먼저 박스 안에 주어진 단어의 의미가 파악되어야 한다. 문장은 2형식과 3형식이다.

The (1) car was (2). It really made (3) noises. Ted bought it (4) for his (5). He thinks a(n) (6) will help it.

1. new/ fast/ old
2. cheap/ expensive/ noisy
3. awful/ different/ funny
4. on credit/ for cash/ on the installment
5. job/ vacation/ son
6. tune-up/ warm up/ oil change

Rewriting

Read the paragraph. Then write the summary of the paragraph with the help of words and phrases in the boxes. (Summaries will vary.)

> **Point**
>
> 먼저 주어진 단락을 주의깊게 읽는다. 그리고 박스 안에 주어진 단어를 사용하여 읽었던 단락을 요약(summary)하여 요약문을 작성한다. 요약문은 3개의 문장으로 완성한다. 문장은 1형식, 2형식 그리고 3형식이다. 단락을 읽을 때는 먼저 의미가 파악되어야 하며, 박스 속에 주어진 단어를 연결하여 문장을 만들 때는 문장의 통일성(unity)에 유의해야 한다. 세련된 문장을 작성하기 위해서 공통 관계와 생략법 등을 최대한 활용하면서 문법을 바르게 적용해야 한다. 또한 콤마(comma)와 물음표(question mark), 마침표(period), 그리고 대문자(capital letter) 등 구두점(punctuation) 사용에 유의한다.

Jack left his car with Mike, the mechanic at ACE GARAGE. Mike worked on the car for five hours. First, he fixed an oil leak, and then he replaced all the hoses. After that, he gave the car a tune-up. Now, he's going to work on the brakes. Jack will be a satisfied customer after Mike finishes the work.

1	took/ car/ ACE GARAGE
2	mechanic/ worked on/ for
3	fixed/ things/ and/ will/ satisfied

Summary: _____

Topic: _____

Main idea: _____

Rewrite the paragraph. Put in capital letters, apostrophes, question marks, commas and periods, if necessary.

Point

문장의 시작과 끝을 의미로 찾은 후 마침표(period)와 대문자(capital letter)를 활용하여 문장을 다시 구성한다. 그리고 콤마(comma)와 아포스트로피(apostrophe) 그리고 물음표(question mark)를 이용하여 문장을 완성한다. 대부분의 문장은 1형식과 3형식이다.

david likes to play baseball he doesnt like to play basketball he plays baseball with his friends on saturday mornings david likes to watch baseball games too last sunday there was a big baseball game on television did david watch it he did

Rewriting

107

Number the sentences in the correct time sequence. Then rewrite the sentences as a complete paragraph.

Point

시간순(time order) 방식에 따라 순서에 맞게 번호를 적은 후 의미의 일관성(coherence)과 통일성(unity)을 갖춘 완성된 단락(complete paragraph)을 작성한다. 시간 표시의 부사 first와 last 그리고 장소 표시의 전치사 from에 유의한다. 문장은 1형식, 2형식 그리고 3형식이다.

_____ From the drugstore, he went to the grocery store.
_____ There he got some chicken for his family's dinner.
_____ Tony's first stop was the drugstore.
_____ His last stop was the post office.
_____ He picked up his mother's medicine there.

Rewriting

108

Read the paragraph. Then write the summary of the paragraph with the help of words and phrases in the boxes. (Summaries will vary.)

> **Point**
>
> 먼저 주어진 단락을 주의깊게 읽는다. 그리고 박스 안에 주어진 단어를 사용하여 읽었던 단락을 요약(summary)하여 요약문을 작성한다. 요약문은 2개의 문장으로 완성한다. 문장은 1형식과 3형식이다. 단락을 읽을 때는 먼저 의미가 파악되어야 하며, 박스 속에 주어진 단어를 연결하여 문장을 만들 때는 문장의 통일성(unity)에 유의해야 한다. 세련된 문장을 작성하기 위해서 공통 관계와 생략법 등을 최대한 활용하면서 문법을 바르게 적용해야 한다. 또한 콤마(comma)와 물음표(question mark), 마침표(period), 그리고 대문자(capital letter) 등 구두점(punctuation) 사용에 유의한다.

Ken and her husband have two children. They live with her mother, father and two brothers in a large old house. Ken's mother helps her care for the children and clean the house. They work very well together. Her father helps Ken's husband in his store. When he needs them, Ken's brothers also help. The family lives and works together happily.

1	Ken's/ all/ together/ large/ old
2	each other/ work/ happily

Summary:

Topic:

Main idea:

109

Match the phrases/clauses in column A with those in column B to form sentences. Then rewrite the sentences in order as dialog.

Point

column A와 어울리는 표현을 column B에서 찾아 연결한 후 의미의 일관성(coherence)과 통일성(unity)을 갖춘 완성된 대화문 (complete dialog)을 작성한다. 문장은 1형식, 2형식 그리고 3형식이다.

A	B
___ If this rain freezes,	a. you should leave soon.
___ Well, if they do that,	b. close the roads if it gets too bad.
___ The weather's terrible. If you're leaving,	c. if that happens?
___ What'll you do	d. if it clears up.
___ I expect to leave at noon	e. I'll stop until it clears up.
___ Yes, but the police will	f. it'll be dangerous to drive.

Rewriting

A:

B:

A:

B:

A:

B:

11o

Read the paragraph and then change it from past tense to present tense. Underline the words that need to be changed. Rewrite the changed paragraph.

Point

과거시제(past tense)를 현재시제(present tense)로 바꿔 각각의 문장을 다시 작성한다. 먼저 전환이 필요한 단어에 밑줄을 긋는다. 가능한 경우 미래시제(future tense)로 바꿔 학습한다. 또한 인칭에도 변화를 주어서 다양한 형태의 문장을 학습한다. 문장은 1형식, 2형식 그리고 3형식이다.

Mr. Brown and his grandson had a very special friendship. Tim was very special to Mr. Brown because he was such a smart boy. He always had a smile on his face and a pleasant word for everyone. The boy and the old man spent many hours together fishing in the lake near their home. When Tim got sick, Mr. Brown was worried.

Rewriting

Read the paragraph. Then write the summary of the paragraph with the help of words and phrases in the boxes. (Summaries will vary.)

> **Point**
>
> 먼저 주어진 단락을 주의깊게 읽는다. 그리고 박스 안에 주어진 단어를 사용하여 읽었던 단락을 요약(summary)하여 요약문을 작성한다. 요약문은 2개의 문장으로 완성한다. 문장은 3형식이다. 단락을 읽을 때는 먼저 의미가 파악되어야 하며, 박스 속에 주어진 단어를 연결하여 문장을 만들 때는 문장의 통일성(unity)에 유의해야 한다. 세련된 문장을 작성하기 위해서 공통 관계와 생략법 등을 최대한 활용하면서 문법을 바르게 적용해야 한다. 또한 콤마(comma)와 물음표(question mark), 마침표(period), 그리고 대문자(capital letter) 등 구두점(punctuation) 사용에 유의한다.

Karen is a cashier in a hotel restaurant. She adds up the checks and takes the money from the customers after they eat. She thinks her job is interesting, and she likes it. People from many places around the world come to eat in the restaurant. Karen enjoys meeting them. She hopes that one day she will be able to take a vacation in their countries.

1	Karen/ job/ because / meets/ interesting/ from/ different/ around
2	hopes/ visit/ countries/ one day

Summary:

Topic:

Main idea:

112

Listen to the paragraph. And dictate the paragraph you listened to using words and the phrases in the box.

Point

먼저 들려주는 지문을 주의깊게 듣는다. 그리고 박스 안에 주어진 단어를 이용하여 들었던 지문과 같은 지문을 작성한다. 지문을 들을 때는 먼저 의미가 파악되어야 하며, 박스 속에 주어진 단어를 연결하여 문장을 만들 때는 문장의 통일성(unity)에 유의한다. 특히 들을 때 잘 들리지 않는 관사, 조동사 will, 전치사 to와 in 등에 유의하여 문법적으로 바른 문장을 작성해야 한다. 또한 콤마(comma)와 물음표(question mark), 마침표(period), 그리고 대문자(capital letter) 등 구두점(punctuation) 사용에 유의한다. 문장은 3형식이다.

Mary/ same thing/ when/ comes home/ evenings
picks up/ mail/ before/ goes into/ house
doesn't open/ until/ changes/ clothes
reads/ mail/ before/ turns on/ TV
when/ finishes/ with/ mail/ cooks
then/ eats/ dinner/ while/ TV

Writing

113

Listen to the paragraph. Write a title then rewrite a similar paragraph using the words and the phrases in the boxes. (Answers will vary.)

Point

먼저 들려주는 지문을 주의깊게 듣는다. 그리고 박스 안에 주어진 단어를 이용하여 들었던 지문과 유사한(similar) 지문과 제목(title)을 작성한다. 지문을 들을 때는 먼저 의미가 파악되어야 하며, 박스 속에 주어진 단어를 연결하여 문장을 만들 때는 문장의 통일성(unity)에 유의한다. 특히 들을 때 잘 들리지 않는 관사, 조동사 will, 전치사 to와 in 등에 유의하여 문법적으로 바른 문장을 작성해야 한다. 또한 콤마(comma)와 물음표(question mark), 마침표(period), 그리고 대문자(capital letter) 등 구두점(punctuation) 사용에 유의한다. 문장은 2형식, 3형식 그리고 4형식(bet동사의 용법)이다.

1	one day/ bet/ basketball
2	bet/ friend/ dollars/ son's/ high school/ beat/ team
3	won/ because/ won
4	proud/ my son's goal/ the game

Title :

Rewriting

Read the paragraph. Then write the summary of the paragraph with the help of words and phrases in the boxes. (Summaries will vary.)

Point

먼저 주어진 단락을 주의깊게 읽는다. 그리고 박스 안에 주어진 단어를 사용하여 읽었던 단락을 요약(summary)하여 요약문을 작성한다. 요약문은 2개의 문장으로 완성한다. 문장은 2형식과 5형식(make동사의 용법)이다. 단락을 읽을 때는 먼저 의미가 파악되어야 하며, 박스 속에 주어진 단어를 연결하여 문장을 만들 때는 문장의 통일성(unity)에 유의해야 한다. 세련된 문장을 작성하기 위해서 공통 관계와 생략법 등을 최대한 활용하면서 문법을 바르게 적용해야 한다. 또한 콤마(comma)와 물음표(question mark), 마침표(period), 그리고 대문자(capital letter) 등 구두점(punctuation) 사용에 유의한다.

Newspapers are important to Alex. He wants to know the local news and the news from around the world. He gets a morning paper and an evening paper. Every day he reads both of these papers. He also reads the business news. He thinks that he's a good businessman because he knows the news of the world and his city.

1	keeping up with/ and/ news/ important/ Alex
2	thinks/ makes/ good businessman

Summary: _____

_____

_____

Topic: _____

Main idea: _____

115

Make questions using words or phrases in the box. (Answers will vary.)

> **Point**
>
> 조동사(auxiliary)를 활용한 4형식 의문문을 만든다. 의미에 맞게 조동사를 선택해야 하며 또한 동사에 따른 직접목적어(direct object)의 선택에 유의하여 문장을 완성한다.

• Can you bring me some fruits?

| Can
Did
Do
Does
Will
Would | I
you
Bill
he
Mary
she
Bob and Al
they
the florist
the waiter | bring
give
mail
sell
send
buy | us
me
you
Tom
him
Pam
her
them
Bill and me
Jan and Ted | some flowers?
some desserts?
some stamps?
a cup of tea?
this jacket?
a letter?
that package?
some fruits?
those books?
a postcard?
the check? |

Writing *ex* Will they send Pam that package?

1.
2.
3.
4.
5.

116

Rewrite the paragraph. Put in capital letters, question marks, commas and periods, if necessary.

Point

문장의 시작과 끝을 의미로 찾은 후 마침표(period)와 대문자(capital letter)를 활용하여 문장을 다시 구성한다. 그리고 콤마(comma)와 물음표(question mark)를 이용하여 문장을 완성한다. 대부분의 문장은 1형식, 2형식 그리고 3형식이다.

---

ann went to a clothing store last week she bought a blue coat for the winter she wants to wear the coat to the october dance she has a blue dress and blue shoes ann went to the store again this morning she bought gloves what color are her gloves are they blue too

Rewriting

117

Read the paragraph and then change it from present tense to past tense. Underline the words that need to be changed. Rewrite the changed paragraph.

Point

현재시제(present tense)를 과거시제(past tense)로 바꿔 각각의 문장을 다시 작성한다. 먼저 전환이 필요한 단어에 밑줄을 긋는다. 가능한 경우 미래시제(future tense)로 바꿔 학습한다. 또한 인칭에도 변화를 주어서 다양한 형태의 문장을 학습한다. 문장은 1형식과 3형식이다.

Mr. Smith gets up at 8 o'clock on Saturday. He sleeps later because he doesn't have to go to work. After he gets dressed, he eats breakfast. He has two eggs, toast, and coffee. After breakfast, he goes to the gym. Then, he goes home and watches TV. About 19:30, he cooks his dinner. Then, he calls his friend, Andy, and makes plans for the evening.

Rewriting

118

Number the sentences in the correct time sequence. Then rewrite the sentences as a complete paragraph.

> **Point**
>
> 시간순(time order) 방식에 따라 순서에 맞게 번호를 적은 후 의미의 일관성(coherence)과 통일성(unity)을 갖춘 완성된 단락(complete paragraph)을 작성한다. 시간 표시의 부사 after와 last 등에 유의한다. 문장은 1형식과 3형식이다.

_____ We ordered some ice cream there.
_____ Last night our family had an early dinner.
_____ After dinner, we went to a movie.
_____ We ate our ice cream in the bar.
_____ After the movie, we stopped at the snack bar.

Rewriting

119

Match the phrases/clauses in column A with those in column B to form sentences. Then rewrite the sentences in order as one paragraph.

Point

column A와 어울리는 표현을 column B에서 찾아 연결한 후 시간순(time order) 그리고 논리순(logical order) 방식에 따라 순서를 정한다. 의미의 일관성(coherence)과 통일성(unity)을 갖춘 완성된 단락(complete paragraph)을 작성한다. 문장은 1형식, 2형식 그리고 3형식이다.

A	B
____ Mark's car started	a. flat!
____ He got out of the car	b. and looked at his tire.
____ He jacked up the car	c. to pull to the right.
____ The car started moving	d. call the garage.
____ Next time, he'll	e. and he fell off the jack.
____ It was	f. and loosened the lugs.

Rewriting

Read the paragraph. Then write the summary of the paragraph with the help of words and phrases in the boxes. (Summaries will vary.)

> **Point**
>
> 먼저 주어진 단락을 주의깊게 읽는다. 그리고 박스 안에 주어진 단어를 사용하여 읽었던 단락을 요약(summary)하여 요약문을 작성한다. 요약문은 3개의 문장으로 완성한다. 문장은 1형식과 2형식이다. 단락을 읽을 때는 먼저 의미가 파악되어야 하며, 박스 속에 주어진 단어를 연결하여 문장을 만들 때는 문장의 통일성(unity)에 유의해야 한다. 세련된 문장을 작성하기 위해서 공통 관계와 생략법 등을 최대한 활용하면서 문법을 바르게 적용해야 한다. 또한 콤마(comma)와 물음표(question mark), 마침표(period), 그리고 대문자(capital letter) 등 구두점(punctuation) 사용에 유의한다.

Hamilton Smith made the first mechanical washing machine in 1858. Before this, people had to wash their clothes by hand. Alva J. Fisher made the first electric washing machine in 1910, which was much easier to use. Washing machines are fantastic because they can wash clothes much faster than people can.

1	first/ machine/ made/ Hamilton Smith
2	1910/ electric/ Alva J. Fisher
3	fantastic/ because/ faster/ people

Summary: _____

_____

Topic: _____

Main idea: _____

121

Match the phrases/clauses in column A with those in column B to form sentences. Then rewrite the sentences in order as one paragraph.

Point

column A와 어울리는 표현을 column B에서 찾아 연결한 후 시간순(time order) 그리고 논리순(logical order) 방식에 따라 순서를 정한다. 의미의 일관성(coherence)과 통일성(unity)을 갖춘 완성된 단락(complete paragraph)을 작성한다. 문장은 1형식과 3형식이다.

A	B
____ The agency made the	a. reservation in Rome for him.
____ First, he went	b. to a travel agency.
____ Roger wanted to take	c. about many places.
____ Thanks to the agency,	d. to go to Rome.
____ He decided	e. a vacation.
____ Then they sent him	f. he could start his vacation in two days.
____ After he picked them up,	g. he went home back.
____ They had information	h. to the airport for his tickets.

Rewriting

122

Read the paragraph; then choose a word for each number. Add the words to the paragraph and rewrite it on the lines below. (Answers will vary.)

> **Point**
>
> 박스 안에 주어진 단어 중 적절한 단어를 번호에 맞게 선택한 후 주어진 문장에 추가하여 좀 더 길고 완벽한 문장을 만드는 학습이다. 이때 주의해야 할 사항은 의미의 일관성(coherence)이다. 먼저 박스 안에 주어진 단어의 의미가 파악되어야 한다.

The (1) girl bought a(n) (2) pencil from the (3) clerk at the fancy store. She took it home and (4) sharpened it. She thought it was a (5) pencil, and she liked it (6).

1. tall/ young/ stupid/ smart
2. new/ big/ cheap/ expensive
3. old/ busy/ nice/ young
4. slowly/ carefully
5. good/ nice/ pretty/ wonderful
6. a lot/ very much

Rewriting

Read the paragraph. Then write the summary of the paragraph with the help of words and phrases in the boxes. (Summaries will vary.)

> **Point**
>
> 먼저 주어진 단락을 주의깊게 읽는다. 그리고 박스 안에 주어진 단어를 사용하여 읽었던 단락을 요약(summary)하여 요약문을 작성한다. 요약문은 3개의 문장으로 완성한다. 문장은 2형식, 3형식 그리고 5형식(have동사의 용법)이다. 단락을 읽을 때는 먼저 의미가 파악되어야 하며, 박스 속에 주어진 단어를 연결하여 문장을 만들 때는 문장의 통일성(unity)에 유의해야 한다. 세련된 문장을 작성하기 위해서 공통 관계와 생략법 등을 최대한 활용하면서 문법을 바르게 적용해야 한다. 또한 콤마(comma)와 물음표(question mark), 마침표(period), 그리고 대문자(capital letter) 등 구두점(punctuation) 사용에 유의한다.

Newspapers are important because they contain a lot of information. Millions of people read newspapers every day, but how do they get their newspapers? There are different ways. One way is to buy it at a newsstand or at a store. Another way is to get it from a vending machine. A third way is to have it brought to their homes.

1	newspapers/ millions of/ every day
2	get/ three ways
3	get/ from a newsstand/ store/ or/ vending machine/ have/ brought

Summary:

Topic:

Main idea:

Combine the ideas into some sentences. And then rewrite a paragraph with the new sentences. (Rewritings will vary.)

Point

공통 관계(common relation)와 생략(ellipsis)법을 적용하여 문장을 간소화한다. 먼저 각각의 문장을 읽고 이해한 후 주어와 동사 그리고 목적어의 공통 관계를 파악한다. 그리고 생략법에 따라 문장을 결합한다. 무엇보다 문장의 통일성(unity)에 유의해야 한다. 필요한 경우에 적절한 접속사, 관계 대명사, 전치사, (대)명사, (대)동사, 조동사 그리고 형용사나 부사 등을 사용하여 단락 전체의 의미를 좀 더 명확하게 한다. 그러나 단락의 일관성(coherence)은 유지해야 한다. "/ /" 속에 포함된 문장들을 결합시켜 하나의 문장으로 다시 작성하여 단락을 완성한다. 문장은 1형식과 3형식이다.

/ My girlfriend, Sarah, likes to listen to classical music. She likes to play classical music. // She plays the violin. She plays in an orchestra. // I don't like to listen to classical music. I don't like to play classical music. // I would rather listen to rock music than to classical music. So I never go to classical music concerts. // Sarah plays in classical music concerts. /

Rewriting

125

Listen to the paragraph. And dictate a paragraph you listened to using words and the phrases in the box.

Point

먼저 들려주는 지문을 주의깊게 듣는다. 그리고 박스 안에 주어진 단어를 이용하여 들었던 지문과 같은 지문을 작성한다. 지문을 들을 때는 먼저 의미가 파악되어야 하며, 박스 속에 주어진 단어를 연결하여 문장을 만들 때는 문장의 통일성(unity)에 유의한다. 특히 들을 때 잘 들리지 않는 관사, 조동사 will 전치사 to와 in 등에 유의하여 문법적으로 바른 문장을 작성해야 한다. 또한 콤마(comma)와 물음표(question mark), 마침표(period), 그리고 대문자(capital letter) 등 구두점(punctuation) 사용에 유의한다. 문장은 1형식, 2형식 그리고 3형식이다.

---

and/ three/ sports
people/ like/ do/ in one race
they/ do/ triathlon race
means/ sports
people/ swim/ a mile(1.6km)
then/ ride/ bicycle
run/ three miles(4.8km)
be/ strong/ win

Writing

Listen to the paragraph. Write a title and then rewrite a similar paragraph using the words and the phrases in the boxes. (Answers will vary.)

Point

먼저 들려주는 지문을 주의깊게 듣는다. 그리고 박스 안에 주어진 단어를 이용하여 들었던 지문과 유사한(similar) 지문과 제목(title)을 작성한다. 지문을 들을 때는 먼저 의미가 파악되어야 하며, 박스 속에 주어진 단어를 연결하여 문장을 만들 때는 문장의 통일성(unity)에 유의한다. 특히 들을 때 잘 들리지 않는 관사, 조동사 will, would, 전치사 to와 in 등에 유의하여 문법적으로 바른 문장을 작성해야 한다. 또한 콤마(comma)와 물음표(question mark), 마침표(period), 그리고 대문자(capital letter) 등 구두점(punctuation) 사용에 유의한다. 문장은 2형식과 3형식이다.

1	first candles/ a long time ago
2	thousands/ years ago/ put/ pieces of wood/ burn longer
3	Egyptians/ cloth and grease/ in bowls/ as candles
4	Romans/ first people/ made candles/ like/ today
5	candles/ grease

Title : _____

Rewriting

127

Read the paragraph. Then write the summary of the paragraph with the help of words and phrases in the boxes. (Summaries will vary.)

Point

먼저 주어진 지문을 주의깊게 읽는다. 그리고 박스 안에 주어진 단어를 사용하여 읽었던 단락을 요약(summary)하여 요약문을 작성한다. 요약문은 3개의 문장으로 완성한다. 문장은 1형식과 3형식이다. 단락을 읽을 때는 먼저 의미가 파악되어야 하며, 박스 속에 주어진 단어를 연결하여 문장을 만들 때는 문장의 통일성(unity)에 유의해야 한다. 세련된 문장을 작성하기 위해서 공통 관계와 생략법 등을 최대한 활용하면서 문법을 바르게 적용해야 한다. 또한 콤마(comma)와 물음표(question mark), 마침표(period), 그리고 대문자(capital letter) 등 구두점(punctuation) 사용에 유의한다.

There are things that you should do before you go on vacation. Check your car. Fill it with gas. Take some common tools with you. Always have a jack, a wrench and a spare tire. Don't forget your driver's license and extra change. Drive carefully and fasten your seatbelt. Do these things, and you'll have a good and safe trip.

1	there/ things/ should/ when/ vacation
2	check/ have/ right/ with/ carefully
3	if/ do/ you'll/ good/ safe/ trip

Summary:

Topic:

Main idea:

128

Read the paragraph. Then write the summary of the paragraph with the help of words and phrases in the boxes. (Summaries will vary.)

> **Point**
>
> 먼저 주어진 지문을 주의깊게 읽는다. 그리고 박스 안에 주어진 단어를 사용하여 읽었던 단락을 요약(summary)하여 요약문을 작성한다. 요약문은 4개의 문장으로 완성한다. 문장은 1형식, 2형식 그리고 3형식이다. 단락을 읽을 때는 먼저 의미가 파악되어야 하며, 박스 속에 주어진 단어를 연결하여 문장을 만들 때는 문장의 통일성(unity)에 유의해야 한다. 세련된 문장을 작성하기 위해서 공통 관계와 생략법 등을 최대한 활용하면서 문법을 바르게 적용해야 한다. 또한 콤마(comma)와 물음표(question mark), 마침표(period), 그리고 대문자(capital letter) 등 구두점(punctuation) 사용에 유의한다.

A Korean just moved to the United States. He went to the bank this morning to find out what to do with his money. He learned about savings and checking accounts. With both accounts, he can deposit and withdraw money. The bank clerk showed him how to fill out deposit slips. He feels good about the bank. He knows that his money will be safe there.

1	a Korean/ bank/ learn/ what/ with
2	learned/ savings and checking
3	also/ how to/ deposit slips
4	good/ satisfied

Summary: ....

....

....

Topic: ....

Main idea: ....

129

Read the paragraph. Then write the summary of the paragraph with the help of words and phrases in the boxes. (Summaries will vary.)

> **Point**
>
> 먼저 주어진 지문을 주의깊게 읽는다. 그리고 박스 안에 주어진 단어를 사용하여 읽었던 단락을 요약(summary)하여 요약문을 작성한다. 요약문은 4개의 문장으로 완성한다. 문장은 1형식과 3형식이다. 단락을 읽을 때는 먼저 의미가 파악되어야 하며, 박스 속에 주어진 단어를 연결하여 문장을 만들 때는 문장의 통일성(unity)에 유의해야 한다. 세련된 문장을 작성하기 위해서 공통 관계와 생략법 등을 최대한 활용하면서 문법을 바르게 적용해야 한다. 또한 콤마(comma)와 물음표(question mark), 마침표(period), 그리고 대문자(capital letter) 등 구두점(punctuation) 사용에 유의한다.

Charlie left his room early this morning. He wanted to stop at a car repair shop to check on his car. He had problems with it the day before yesterday. It had overheated that morning on his way to work. The oil pressure gauge had indicated a problem. When he left his car at the repair shop on Thursday, the mechanic told him to stop by on Friday morning.

1	Charlie/ problem/ before yesterday
2	took/ shop/ fixed
3	overheated
4	today/ checking/ if/ ready

Summary: ....

....

Topic: ....

Main idea: ....

13o

Write a paragraph using words and phrases in the boxes. (Answers will vary.)

> **Point**
>
> 박스 안에 주어진 단어를 활용하여 의미에 맞게끔 각각의 문장을 만든다. 핵심은 의미의 완벽한 전달에 있다. 주어의 일치와 소유격 형용사의 일치 그리고 동사와 목적어의 관계를 잘 고려하여 단락(**paragraph**)을 완성한다. 지문(**passage**)은 길지만 모든 문장은 1형식과 3형식이다.

- I went to the bank yesterday. …

Tom and Al Harry Julie I	went to the	drug store department store bank grocery store	yesterday. after lunch. Monday night. this morning.	They He She I
bought	some bread some medicines a money order some fruits a shirt	and	milk. film. traveler's checks. a toothpaste. a comb.	They He She I	wanted to had to
cash a check.		The clerk asked for	Tom's Harry's his Julie's her my	ID card. driver's license. identification.	
But	he she I	did not have it.	It was	at home. in the car. at the hotel.	

Writing *ex* Tom and Al went to the department store yesterday. They bought a shirt and film. ...

1.

2.

3.

4.

5.

131

Rewrite the paragraph with capital letters and periods, if necessary.

Point

문장의 시작과 끝을 의미로 찾은 후 마침표(periods)와 대문자(capital letters)를 활용하여 문장을 다시 구성한다. 대부분의 문장은 1형식과 3형식이다.

> paul likes to take trips he takes two trips every year the first trip is to wyoming he visits his father and his mother his second trip is to a new city he likes to see a new city every year he went to chicago last year he wants to go to new york this year

Rewriting

132

Match the phrases/clauses in column A with those in column B to form sentences. Then rewrite the sentences in order as dialog.

> **Point**
>
> column A와 어울리는 대화를 column B에서 찾아 일관성을 갖춘 대화문(dialog)을 완성한다. 의미의 일관성(coherence)과 통일성(unity)을 갖춘 완성된 대화문을 작성한다. 문장은 1형식, 2형식 그리고 3형식이다.

A	B
____ Instead of the one in L.A.? Why did you do that?	a. I haven't made up my mind yet. I'll have to look at apartments.
____ Where are you going to live in San Francisco?	b. I've decided to take the one in San Francisco.
____ You'll enjoy the university. When do you plan to leave?	c. Because the pay is better, and I can take some courses at the university there.
____ Hi, Sony. What have you decided to do about the job offers?	d. The end of the month.

> **Rewriting**

A : _____   B : _____

A : _____   B : _____

A : _____   B : _____

A : _____   B : _____

133

Read the paragraph; then choose a word for each number. Add the words to the paragraph and rewrite it on the lines below. (Answers will vary.)

Point

박스 안에 주어진 단어 중 적절한 단어를 번호에 맞게 선택한 후 주어진 문장에 추가하여 좀 더 길고 완벽한 문장을 만드는 학습이다. 이때 주의해야 할 사항은 의미의 일관성(coherence)이다. 먼저 박스 안에 주어진 단어의 의미가 파악되어야 한다. 문장은 1형식, 2형식 그리고 3형식이다.

Helen was on vacation. She bought a local (1). She wanted (2) a (3). She was (4), and she wanted (5) before she went back to (6).

1. map/ car/ newspaper
2. to read about/ to drive to/ to find
3. pleasant hotel/ good restaurant/ nice apartment
4. late/ hungry/ lost
5. to get there/ to eat/ to leave
6. her hotel/ her home/ the river

Rewriting

Listen to the paragraph. Write a title and then rewrite a similar paragraph using the words and the phrases in the boxes. (Answers will vary.)

Point

먼저 들려주는 지문을 주의깊게 듣는다. 그리고 박스 안에 주어진 단어를 이용하여 들었던 지문과 유사한(similar) 지문과 제목(title)을 작성한다. 지문을 들을 때는 먼저 의미가 파악되어야 하며, 박스 속에 주어진 단어를 연결하여 문장을 만들 때는 문장의 통일성(unity)에 유의한다. 특히 들을 때 잘 들리지 않는 관사, 조동사 will과 would, 전치사 to와 in 등에 유의하여 문법적으로 바른 문장을 작성해야 한다. 또한 콤마(comma)와 물음표(question mark), 마침표(period), 그리고 대문자(capital letter) 등 구두점(punctuation) 사용에 유의한다. 문장은 1형식, 2형식 그리고 3형식이다.

1	people/ birthday parties/ years
2	first party/ Egypt/ 3,000 years ago
3	pharaoh/ head of the country/ party/ people/ his birthday
4	after this/ had parties/ but only important/ had/ them
5	today/ popular/ many countries

Title :

Rewriting

135

Read the paragraph. Then write the summary of the paragraph with the help of words and phrases in the boxes. (Summaries will vary.)

> **Point**
>
> 먼저 주어진 지문을 주의깊게 읽는다. 그리고 박스 안에 주어진 단어를 사용하여 읽었던 단락을 요약(summary)하여 요약문을 작성한다. 요약문은 2개의 문장으로 완성한다. 문장은 1형식과 2형식이다. 단락을 읽을 때는 먼저 의미가 파악되어야 하며, 박스 속에 주어진 단어를 연결하여 문장을 만들 때는 문장의 통일성(unity)에 유의해야 한다. 세련된 문장을 작성하기 위해서 공통 관계와 생략법 등을 최대한 활용하면서 문법을 바르게 적용해야 한다. 또한 콤마(comma)와 물음표(question mark), 마침표(period), 그리고 대문자(capital letter) 등 구두점(punctuation) 사용에 유의한다.

People get together for different reasons. Friends get together because they enjoy being with each other. Businessmen and businesswomen get together for business meetings because they want to discuss and make decisions about their businesses. People also get together for parties for birthdays, new babies, and other happy things. A get-together can be for fun or business.

1	different/ kinds/ get together/ reasons
2	get-togethers/ be/ fun/ business

Summary:

Topic:

Main idea:

136

Read to the paragraph. Then write the summary of the paragraph with the help of words and phrases in the boxes. (Summaries will vary.)

> **Point**
>
> 먼저 주어진 지문을 주의깊게 읽는다. 그리고 박스 안에 주어진 단어를 사용하여 읽었던 단락을 요약(summary)하여 요약문을 작성한다. 요약문은 2개의 문장으로 완성한다. 문장은 1형식과 3형식이다. 단락을 읽을 때는 먼저 의미가 파악되어야 하며, 박스 속에 주어진 단어를 연결하여 문장을 만들 때는 문장의 통일성(unity)에 유의해야 한다. 세련된 문장을 작성하기 위해서 공통 관계와 생략법 등을 최대한 활용하면서 문법을 바르게 적용해야 한다. 또한 콤마(comma)와 물음표(question mark), 마침표(period), 그리고 대문자(capital letter) 등 구두점(punctuation) 사용에 유의한다.

Commercials are a big part of American TV. There are several commercials every fifteen or twenty minutes. Some of them are funny and entertaining, and some of them are not. Most of them have one purpose: to get you to buy something. Most of us don't like to see commercials when we are watching TV, but because commercials make money for businesses, they are here to stay.

1	there/ a lot/ TV/ most/don't like
2	commercials/ money/ businesses/ so/ here/ stay

Summary:

Topic:

Main idea:

Part III

Advanced Course

137

Write a paragraph with these words. (Answers will vary.)

> **Point**
>
> 박스 안에 주어진 단어를 활용하여 의미에 맞게끔 각각의 문장을 만든다. 핵심은 완벽한 의미 전달에 있다. 주어의 일치와 소유격 형용사의 일치 그리고 부사(구)와 부사(구)와의 관계를 잘 고려하여 단락(paragraph)을 완성한다. 문장은 1형식과 3형식이다.

• Becky went to Korea last week. …

Susan Becky The athletes My boss Tony	went to	Korea Houston Chicago China New York	last week. yesterday. last year.	They She He	traveled by
bus. bike. car. plane. train.	His Their Her	family fans friends men	met	him her them	at the Bank of America. at the station. at the airport. at the hotel. at the restaurant.
They He She	took	them her him	to	their the his her	company. house. hotel. room. restaurant.

Writing

ex The athletes went to Korea last year. They traveled by train. Their fans met them at the station. ...

1.

2.

3.

4.

5.

138

Rewrite the paragraph with capital letters and periods, if necessary.

Point

문장의 시작과 끝을 의미로 찾은 후 마침표(periods)와 대문자(capital letters)를 활용하여 문장을 다시 구성한다. 대부분의 문장은 1형식, 2형식 그리고 3형식이다.

> betty and henry went to a dance last saturday betty wore a long pink dress henry wore a black suit they danced all night long they were very happy they were very sore the next day their feet hurt their arms hurt their heads hurt they slept all morning long they were all right on monday

Rewriting

139

Match the phrases/clauses in column A with those in column B to form sentences. Then rewrite the sentences in order as one paragraph.

> **Point**
>
> column A와 어울리는 표현을 column B에서 찾아 연결한 후 시간순(time order) 그리고 논리순(logical order) 방식에 따라 순서를 정한다. 의미의 일관성(coherence)과 통일성(unity)을 갖춘 완성된 단락(complete paragraph)을 작성한다. 문장은 1형식과 3형식이다.

A	B
___ When do you think	a. or I can go in the winter.
___ I can go in the summer,	b. if I go in the winter.
___ If I go in the summer,	c. decided when to take my vacation yet.
___ But I will enjoy the snow	d. I should go?
___ I haven't	e. I can enjoy the sun at the beach.

Rewriting

Listen to the paragraph. Write a title and then rewrite a similar paragraph using the words and the phrases in the box. (Answers will vary.)

Point

먼저 들려주는 지문을 주의깊게 듣는다. 그리고 박스 안에 주어진 단어를 이용하여 들었던 지문과 유사한(similar) 지문과 제목(title)을 작성한다. 지문을 들을 때는 먼저 의미가 파악되어야 하며, 박스 속에 주어진 단어를 연결하여 문장을 만들 때는 문장의 통일성(unity)에 유의한다. 특히 들을 때 잘 들리지 않는 관사, 조동사 will과 would, 전치사 to와 in 등에 유의하여 문법적으로 바른 문장을 작성해야 한다. 또한 콤마(comma)와 물음표(question mark), 마침표(period), 그리고 대문자(capital letter) 등 구두점(punctuation) 사용에 유의한다. 문장은 3형식이다.

1	spent some time/ patients/ hospital/ last week
2	volunteered/ time
3	visited/ talked/ took/ lunches/ them
4	good time/ want/ again/ next

Title :

Rewriting

141

Read the paragraph. Then write the summary of the paragraph with the help of words and phrases in the boxes.(Summaries will vary.)

> **Point**
>
> 먼저 주어진 단락을 주의깊게 읽는다. 그리고 박스 안에 주어진 단어를 사용하여 읽었던 단락을 요약(summary)하여 요약문을 작성한다. 요약문은 2개의 문장으로 완성한다. 문장은 1형식과 3형식이다. 단락을 읽을 때는 먼저 의미가 파악되어야 하며, 박스 속에 주어진 단어를 연결하여 문장을 만들 때는 문장의 통일성(unity)에 유의해야 한다. 세련된 문장을 작성하기 위해서 공통 관계와 생략법 등을 최대한 활용하면서 문법을 바르게 적용해야 한다. 또한 콤마(comma)와 물음표(question mark), 마침표(period), 그리고 대문자(capital letter) 등 구두점(punctuation) 사용에 유의한다.

Garages usually give guarantees with most of their work. The mechanics want satisfied customers. They'll work on your car; then they'll work on it again without a charge when there's still a problem. Customers are unhappy when they have to pay for the same thing two times. A dissatisfied customer will usually not return, and he'll also tell all of his friends that they shouldn't go to that garage.

1	garages/ guarantee/ because/ not/ want/ lose/ customers
2	most/ unhappy/ not/ return

Summary:

Topic:

Main idea:

Listen to the paragraph. Write a title and then rewrite a similar paragraph using the words and the phrases in the boxes. (Answers will vary.)

Point

먼저 들려주는 지문을 주의깊게 듣는다. 그리고 박스 안에 주어진 단어를 이용하여 들었던 지문과 유사한(similar) 지문과 제목(title)을 작성한다. 지문을 들을 때는 먼저 의미가 파악되어야 하며, 박스 속에 주어진 단어를 연결하여 문장을 만들 때는 문장의 통일성(unity)에 유의한다. 특히 들을 때 잘 들리지 않는 관사, 조동사 will과 would, 전치사 to와 in 등에 유의하여 문법적으로 바른 문장을 작성해야 한다. 또한 콤마(comma)와 물음표(question mark), 마침표(period), 그리고 대문자(capital letter) 등 구두점(punctuation) 사용에 유의한다. 문장은 2형식과 3형식이다.

1	pain/ his back
2	worse/ a few hours
3	called/ doctor
4	the doctor/ should operation
5	operated/ on/ afternoon

Title : ....

Rewriting

....
....
....
....

143

Read the paragraph. Then write the summary of the paragraph with the help of words and phrases in the boxes. (Summaries will vary.)

> **Point**
>
> 먼저 주어진 지문을 주의깊게 읽는다. 그리고 박스 안에 주어진 단어를 사용하여 읽었던 단락을 요약(summary)하여 요약문을 작성한다. 요약문은 2개의 문장으로 완성한다. 문장은 1형식과 2형식이다. 단락을 읽을 때는 먼저 의미가 파악되어야 하며, 박스 속에 주어진 단어를 연결하여 문장을 만들 때는 문장의 통일성(unity)에 유의해야 한다. 세련된 문장을 작성하기 위해서 공통 관계와 생략법 등을 최대한 활용하면서 문법을 바르게 적용해야 한다. 또한 콤마(comma)와 물음표(question mark), 마침표(period), 그리고 대문자(capital letter) 등 구두점(punctuation) 사용에 유의한다.

People who are driving on long trips should stop often. They can buy gas, eat, sightsee, or just exercise a little. When they get tired, they can pull over to the side of the road and rest. Without regular breaks, drivers can easily become tired or careless. Sometimes when a driver falls asleep at the wheel, his vehicle leaves the road or crosses into the opposite lane and causes a terrible accident.

| 1 | drivers/ stop/ regularly/ long trips |
| 2 | those who/ breaks/ can/ tired/ cause |

Summary:

Topic:

Main idea:

Make perfect sentences using the words in the boxes. (Answers will vary.)

Point

박스 안에 주어진 단어를 활용하여 의미에 맞게끔 각각의 문장을 만든다. 핵심은 의미의 완벽한 전달에 있다. 주어의 일치와 목적어, 부사구의 일치에 유의하면서 단락(paragraph)을 완성한다. to 부정사의 용법은 '목적(~하기 위하여)'을 나타내며 문장은 3형식이다.

• Paula has a new car. …

Paula Sony My parents Mark Ben and I	has have	a new	car. radio refrigerator. couch.	They She We He	keep keeps
it	in the	garage. bedroom. living room. kitchen.	We She They He	uses use	it	to	drive keep listen sit
to food on.		cold. music. school. work.			

Writing   *ex*   Paula has a new refrigerator. She keeps it in the kitchen. …

1. _____

2. _____

3. _____

4. _____

5. _____

145

Rewrite the paragraph. Put in capital letters, apostrophes, commas, quotation marks, question marks, exclamation marks and periods, if necessary.

Point

문장의 시작과 끝을 의미로 찾은 후 마침표(period)와 대문자(capital letter)를 활용하여 문장을 다시 구성한다. 그리고 콤마(comma), 아포스트로피(apostrophe), 물음표(question mark), 따옴표(quotation mark), 느낌표(exclamation mark)를 이용하여 문장을 완성한다. 대부분의 문장은 1형식, 2형식 그리고 3형식이다.

saturday morning harry made a long distance phone call to his family his mother answered the phone harry said hi mom how are you she said harry its harry on the phone then harrys father his brother and his brothers wife picked up the phone they talked for about ten minutes

Rewriting

Read the paragraph and then change it from the past tense to the future tense. Underline the other parts of the paragraph that need changing. Rewrite the changed paragraph.

Point

과거시제(past tense)를 미래시제(future tense)로 바꿔 각각의 문장을 다시 작성한다. 먼저 전환이 필요한 단어에 밑줄을 긋는다. 가능한 경우에 과거시제를 현재시제, 미래 진행형 등으로 전환시켜 다양한 형태의 문장을 학습한다. 문장은 1형식과 3형식이다.

> Mr. and Mrs. Clinton took their vacation last month. They drove to Canada with some friends. The drive to Canada took four days. They stayed in some very nice motels on the way. They ate at some wonderful restaurants; they danced to some nice music; and they saw some beautiful things.

Rewriting

147

Number the sentences in the correct time sequence. Then rewrite the sentences as a complete paragraph.

Point

시간순(time order) 방식에 따라 순서에 맞게 번호를 적은 후 의미의 일관성(coherence)과 통일성(unity)을 갖춘 완성된 단락(complete paragraph)을 작성한다. 논리적 전개는 물론 시간 표시의 접속사 after와 then에 유의한다. 문장은 1형식과 3형식이다.

_____ After he signed the letter, he put it in the envelope.
_____ Then he put a stamp on the envelope and left with the letter in his hand.
_____ Jerry wrote a letter to his friend yesterday.
_____ He went to the post office and mailed the letter.
_____ Then he wrote his friend's address on the back of the envelope and his return address on the front.

Rewriting

148

Match the phrases/clauses in column A with those in column B to form sentences. Then rewrite the sentences in order as one paragraph.

Point

column A와 어울리는 표현을 column B에서 찾아 연결한 후 시간순(time order) 그리고 논리순(logical order) 방식에 따라 순서를 정한다. 의미의 일관성(coherence)과 통일성(unity)을 갖춘 완성된 단락(complete paragraph)을 작성한다. 문장은 1형식과, 3형식 그리고 5형식(hang동사의 용법)이다.

A	B
____ They had	a. some pretty ones.
____ I needed some drapes	b. and decided to go shopping.
____ I went to	c. for the bedroom.
____ I woke up this morning	d. WHITES department store.
____ I bought them, took them home,	e. and hung them up.

Rewriting

Read the paragraph; then choose a word for each number. Add the words to the paragraph and rewrite it on the lines below. (Answers will vary.)

Point

박스 안에 주어진 단어 중 적절한 단어를 번호에 맞게 선택한 후 주어진 문장에 추가하여 좀 더 길고 완벽한 문장을 만드는 학습이다. 이때 주의해야 할 사항은 의미의 일관성(coherence)이다. 먼저 박스 안에 주어진 단어의 의미가 파악되어야 한다. 문장은 1형식, 2형식 그리고 3형식이다.

(1) roommate is a (2) man. He works out at the (3) gym every day. (4), he takes (5) gym clothes with him. But yesterday, he forgot, and he had to borrow (6) clothes.

1. My/ Our/ John's/ His
2. young/ strong/ healthy/ weak
3. downtown/ men's/ school/ company
4. Most of the time/ Sometimes/ Usually/ Always
5. his/ clean/ some/ my
6. some/ someone's/ a friend's/ my

Rewriting

15o

Combine the ideas into some sentences. And then rewrite a paragraph with the new sentences. (Rewritings will vary.)

Point

공통 관계(common relation)와 생략(ellipsis)법을 적용하여 문장을 간소화한다. 먼저 각각의 문장을 읽고 이해한 후 주어와 동사 그리고 목적어의 공통 관계를 파악한다. 그리고 생략법에 따라 문장을 결합한다. 무엇보다 문장의 통일성(unity)에 유의해야 한다. 필요한 경우에 적절한 접속사, 관계 대명사, 전치사, (대)명사, (대)동사, 조동사 그리고 형용사나 부사 등을 사용하여 단락 전체의 의미를 좀 더 명확하게 한다. 그러나 단락의 일관성(coherence)은 유지해야 한다. "/ /" 속에 포함된 문장들을 결합시켜 하나의 문장으로 다시 작성하여 단락을 완성한다. 문장은 2형식과 3형식이다.

/ Captain Jackson behaves with honor. He does what is right. // He salutes senior officers. He salutes junior officers. He treats senior and junior officers with respect. // He does not break the rules. He obeys the rules. He does what he is told by his seniors. // He gives reasonable orders. He treats subordinates with respect. // Maybe Captain Jackson will be the chief of a police station someday. /

Rewriting

151

Listen to the paragraph. Write a title and then rewrite a similar paragraph using the words and the phrases in the boxes. (Answers will vary.)

Point

먼저 들려주는 지문을 주의깊게 듣는다. 그리고 박스 안에 주어진 단어를 이용하여 들었던 지문과 유사한(similar) 지문과 제목(title)을 작성한다. 지문을 들을 때는 먼저 의미가 파악되어야 하며, 박스 속에 주어진 단어를 연결하여 문장을 만들 때는 문장의 통일성(unity)에 유의한다. 특히 들을 때 잘 들리지 않는 관사, 조동사 will과 would, 전치사 to와 in 등에 유의하여 문법적으로 바른 문장을 작성해야 한다. 또한 콤마(comma)와 물음표(question mark), 마침표(period), 그리고 대문자(capital letter) 등 구두점(punctuation) 사용에 유의한다. 문장은 2형식과 3형식이다.

1	Paul/ aunt/ day
2	used to/ bread/ cakes
3	would/ also/ delicious
4	used to/ recipes/ give/ friends
5	loved/ very much
6	wonderful

Title : _____

Rewriting

152

Read the paragraph. Then write the summary of the paragraph with the help of words and phrases in the boxes. (Summaries will vary.)

> **Point**
>
> 먼저 주어진 지문을 주의깊게 읽는다. 그리고 박스 안에 주어진 단어를 사용하여 읽었던 단락을 요약(summary)하여 요약문을 작성한다. 요약문은 2개의 문장으로 완성한다. 문장은 2형식, 3형식 그리고 4형식(offer동사의 용법)이다. 단락을 읽을 때는 먼저 의미가 파악되어야 하며, 박스 속에 주어진 단어를 연결하여 문장을 만들 때는 문장의 통일성(unity)에 유의해야 한다. 세련된 문장을 작성하기 위해서 공통 관계와 생략법 등을 최대한 활용하면서 문법을 바르게 적용해야 한다. 또한 콤마(comma)와 물음표(question mark), 마침표(period), 그리고 대문자(capital letter) 등 구두점(punctuation) 사용에 유의한다.

From the beginning of time, man has been interested in the ocean but a little frightened of things on the bottom of it. The bottom of the ocean is a place that many people think that it is cold, black, and dangerous. We don't know much about the bottom of the ocean, but today we have new tools so we can study the animals and plants that live there. The ocean may offer the world food and perhaps even a place to live in the future.

1	man/ interested/ ocean/ long time/ but/ about/ ocean
2	today/ tools/ study/ offer /world/ things/ future

Summary:

Topic:

Main idea:

153

Read the paragraph. Then write the summary of the paragraph with the help of words and phrases in the boxes. (Summaries will vary.)

> **Point**
>
> 먼저 주어진 지문을 주의깊게 읽는다. 그리고 박스 안에 주어진 단어를 사용하여 읽었던 단락을 요약(summary)하여 요약문을 작성한다. 요약문은 2개의 문장으로 완성한다. 문장은 1형식과 3형식이다. 단락을 읽을 때는 먼저 의미가 파악되어야 하며, 박스 속에 주어진 단어를 연결하여 문장을 만들 때는 문장의 통일성(unity)에 유의해야 한다. 세련된 문장을 작성하기 위해서 공통 관계와 생략법 등을 최대한 활용하면서 문법을 바르게 적용해야 한다. 또한 콤마(comma)와 물음표(question mark), 마침표(period), 그리고 대문자(capital letter) 등 구두점(punctuation) 사용에 유의한다.

Many people get the flu in the winter. Some people feel bad for just two or three days, and others are sick for much longer. The symptoms of the flu are usually fever, headache, backache, a runny nose, and sometimes a cough. Take some medicine for the pain and fever and drink a lot of fruit juice. When you have the flu, you can't do much. Just stay home and get a lot of rest.

1	flu/ lasts/ few/ or longer/ and/ variety/ symptoms
2	medicine/ rest/ help/ when/ have

Summary:

Topic:

Main idea:

154

Listen to the paragraph and then read and answer the questions with the help of words and phrases in the boxes. Finally, write a paragraph similar to the one you listened to using the answers.

> **Point**
>
> 먼저 들려주는 지문을 주의깊게 듣는다. 이때 지문 전체의 의미 파악이 중요하다. 다음 박스에 주어진 단어를 활용하여 주어진 질문에 대한 답을 작성한다. 그리고 마지막으로 답을 서로 결합하여 의미의 일관성(coherence)과 문장의 통일성(unity)을 갖춘 지문을 완성한다. 이때 각 문장에 문법적인 오류가 없도록 유의한다. 듣기 능력(listening ability)과 문법 지식(grammar knowledge)을 배양시키는 학습이다. 문장은 3형식이다.

Questions:

1. What did the people at North Dakota University study?
2. Which group of people changes its mind more often?
3. Which group takes a longer time to make a decision?
4. Which group stays with its decisions longer?

1	people/ university/ decisions of men and women
2	men/ change/ minds/ more often
3	women/ longer/ make/ decision
4	women/ stay/ decisions/ than

Answers

1.
2.
3.
4.

Rewriting

155

Read the paragraph. Then write the summary of the paragraph with the help of words and phrases in the boxes. (Summaries will vary.)

> **Point**
>
> 먼저 주어진 지문을 주의깊게 읽는다. 그리고 박스 안에 주어진 단어를 사용하여 읽었던 단락을 요약(summary)하여 요약문을 작성한다. 요약문은 2개의 문장으로 완성한다. 문장은 2형식이다. 단락을 읽을 때는 먼저 의미가 파악되어야 하며, 박스 속에 주어진 단어를 연결하여 문장을 만들 때는 문장의 통일성(unity)에 유의해야 한다. 세련된 문장을 작성하기 위해서 공통 관계와 생략법 등을 최대한 활용하면서 문법을 바르게 적용해야 한다. 또한 콤마(comma)와 물음표(question mark), 마침표(period), 그리고 대문자(capital letter) 등 구두점(punctuation) 사용에 유의한다.

When you buy clothes in another country, it can be a problem. Different countries use different measurements for their clothes. Most countries use metric measurements, but the United States uses feet and inches. In other countries that use the same measurements, the sizes are still a little different. That's because most countries use the average height, shape, and weight of their people for their sizes. You may think you know the size you want, but remember it's always best to try on clothes before you buy them.

1	sizes/ clothes/ different/ each/ because/ country/ average/ its own people
2	so / when/ in another country/ best/ try on/ before/ buy

Summary:

Topic:

Main idea:

156

Read the paragraph. Then write the summary of the paragraph with the help of words and phrases in the boxes. (Summaries will vary.)

> **Point**
>
> 먼저 주어진 지문을 주의깊게 읽는다. 그리고 박스 안에 주어진 단어를 사용하여 읽었던 단락을 요약(summary)하여 요약문을 작성한다. 요약문은 2개의 문장으로 완성한다. 문장은 1형식과 3형식이다. 단락을 읽을 때는 먼저 의미가 파악되어야 하며, 박스 속에 주어진 단어를 연결하여 문장을 만들 때는 문장의 통일성(unity)에 유의해야 한다. 세련된 문장을 작성하기 위해서 공통 관계와 생략법 등을 최대한 활용하면서 문법을 바르게 적용해야 한다. 또한 콤마(comma)와 물음표(question mark), 마침표(period), 그리고 대문자(capital letter) 등 구두점(punctuation) 사용에 유의한다.

Many stones that look like diamonds are not natural diamonds. They are made of glass. These glass stones look very much like diamonds, but they are not as hard as real diamonds, and they don't sparkle like real diamonds. People use these stones in jewelry when they can't afford real diamonds. A professional jewelery can tell the difference between the stones and the diamonds with just a glance but other people will probably have a hard time telling the difference.

1	there/ glass/ stones/ look like/ which/ jewelry/ afford/ diamonds
2	professional/ tell/ difference/ stones/ diamonds/ with/ quick look/ but

Summary:

Topic:

Main idea:

157

Sequence the sentences. Then add a connective and rewrite a paragraph.

Point

시간순 (time order)을 나타내는 연결사(connectives)들의 의미를 먼저 파악한다. 그리고 주어진 문장을 시간과 논리적 방식에 따라 순서에 맞게 번호를 적은 후 주어진 연결사 중 바른 연결사를 추가하여 의미의 일관성(coherence)과 통일성(unity)을 갖춘 완성된 단락(complete paragraph)을 작성한다. 문장은 1형식과 3형식이다.

CONNECTIVE WORDS
at last/ next/ first/ then
after that/ finally/ following that

_____ I picked out the best and checked them out.
_____ I selected books about the atmosphere.
_____ I looked at the books I had selected.
_____ I went to the library the other day.
_____ With my arms filled with books, I went back to my room to start my research.

Rewriting

158

Match the phrases/clauses in column A with those in column B to form sentences. Then rewrite the sentences in order as one paragraph.

Point

column A와 어울리는 표현을 column B에서 찾아 연결한 후 시간순(time order) 그리고 논리순(logical order) 방식에 따라 순서를 정한다. 의미의 일관성(coherence)과 통일성(unity)을 갖춘 완성된 단락(complete paragraph)을 작성한다. 문장은 1형식, 2형식 그리고 3형식이다.

A	B
___ He drove to the nearest house and used the telephone there ___ He thought he was the only person on the highway, but when he came to the top of a hill, ___ Then Mr. Brown ___ Mr. Brown was driving home from ___ He tried to return to the accident because he was worried about the people who might be hurt,	a. really began to worry. b. but he couldn't find it again; the cars weren't there anymore. c. work one dark, rainy night. d. to call the police. e. he saw that there was an accident on the road ahead.

Rewriting

159

Read the paragraph; then choose a word for each number. Add the words to the paragraph and rewrite it on the lines below. (Answers will vary.)

Point

박스 안에 주어진 단어 중 적절한 단어를 번호에 맞게 선택한 후 주어진 문장에 추가하여 좀 더 길고 완벽한 문장을 만드는 학습이다. 이때 주의해야 할 사항은 의미의 일관성(coherence)이다. 먼저 박스 안에 주어진 단어의 의미가 파악되어야 한다. 문장은 1형식, 2형식 그리고 3형식이다.

Paul needed some (1). He went to the (2), but it was (3). He asked a man for some (4). The man said, "Use the (5) for (6) or (7)."

1. money/ food/ books
2. library/ store/ bank
3. closed/ open/ crowded
4. advice/ food/ newspapers
5. paper/ machine/ salad
6. dessert/ dictionary/ withdrawals
7. cakes/ library books/ deposits

Rewriting

160

Listen to the paragraph and then listen to the questions with the help of words and phrases in the boxes. Finally, write a paragraph similar to the one you listened to using the answer.

Point

먼저 들려주는 지문을 주의깊게 듣는다. 이때 지문 전체의 의미 파악이 중요하다. 다음 박스에 주어진 단어를 활용하여 주어진 질문에 대한 답을 작성한다. 그리고 마지막으로 답을 서로 결합하여 의미의 일관성(coherence)과 문장의 통일성(unity)을 갖춘 지문을 완성하며, 문법적으로 오류가 없도록 유의한다. 듣기 능력(listening ability)과 문법 지식(grammar knowledge)을 배양시키는 학습이다. 문장은 1형식과 3형식이다.

Questions:

1. What are two things people spend when they try to lose weight?
2. Where do they go to lose weight?
3. How else do they try to lose weight?
4. What do they do at a health club?
5. What may each person have?

1	spend/ time/ money/ when/ try
2	go /expensive/ clubs
3	try/ unusual
4	at/ follow/ careful/ daily
5	everyone/ special/ exercise plan

Answers

1.

2.

3.

4.

5.

Rewriting

Read the paragraph. Then write the summary of the paragraph with the help of words and phrases in the boxes. (Summaries will vary.)

> **Point**
>
> 먼저 주어진 지문을 주의깊게 읽는다. 그리고 박스 안에 주어진 단어를 사용하여 읽었던 단락을 요약(summary)하여 요약문을 작성한다. 요약문은 2개의 문장으로 완성한다. 문장은 1형식(there구문)과 4형식(tell동사의 용법)이다. 단락을 읽을 때는 먼저 의미가 파악되어야 하며, 박스 속에 주어진 단어를 연결하여 문장을 만들 때는 문장의 통일성(unity)에 유의해야 한다. 세련된 문장을 작성하기 위해서 공통 관계와 생략법 등을 최대한 활용하면서 문법을 바르게 적용해야 한다. 또한 콤마(comma)와 물음표(question mark), 마침표(period), 그리고 대문자(capital letter) 등 구두점(punctuation) 사용에 유의한다.

On winter nights, accidents often take place because a driver doesn't know if there is ice or snow on the road. Now there is a new item that tells a driver the temperature of the road ahead. This tells him if there might be ice or snow on the road. The new item is made of a material that changes color with the temperature. It's put on a wood or metal pole next to the road, and a driver can see the color thanks to the car's headlights. Green shows temperatures above 45 degrees F, yellow shows temperatures around 37 degrees F, and orange and red show lower temperatures.

1	there/ a new item/ prevent/ accidents
2	tells/ temperature/ road ahead/ and/ if/ might/ ice or snow

Summary:

Topic:

Main idea:

Read the paragraph. Then write the summary of the paragraph with the help of words and phrases in the boxes. (Summaries will vary.)

> **Point**
>
> 먼저 주어진 지문을 주의깊게 읽는다. 그리고 박스 안에 주어진 단어를 사용하여 읽었던 단락을 요약(summary)하여 요약문을 작성한다. 요약문은 2개의 문장으로 완성한다. 문장은 3형식이다. 단락을 읽을 때는 먼저 의미가 파악되어야 하며, 박스 속에 주어진 단어를 연결하여 문장을 만들 때는 문장의 통일성(unity)에 유의해야 한다. 세련된 문장을 작성하기 위해서 공통 관계와 생략법 등을 최대한 활용하면서 문법을 바르게 적용해야 한다. 또한 콤마(comma)와 물음표(question mark), 마침표(period), 그리고 대문자(capital letter) 등 구두점(punctuation) 사용에 유의한다.

When you are in a store, a school, an office, or an apartment, look up at the ceiling. You may see small metal plates up there, and this should make you feel safer. These plates spray water and chemicals when there is a fire in a room or building. At the same time, an alarm goes off, making aloud noise. This alarm tells the people to get out of the building. It also lets the fire department know where the fire is. These small metal plates can help to save lives.

1	metal/ plates/ ceilings /buildings/ spray/ put out
2	alarms/ call/ department

Summary:

Topic:

Main idea:

163

Make a paragraph using the words and phrases in the boxes. (Answers will vary.)

Point

박스 안에 주어진 단어를 활용하여 의미에 맞게끔 각각의 문장을 만든다. 핵심은 의미의 일관성(coherence)과 통일성(unity)에 있다. 주어의 일치와 목적어, 부사구의 일치에 유의하며 빈도부사를 적절히 활용하여 단락(paragraph)을 완성한다. 지문(passage)은 길지만 문장은 1형식과 2형식 그리고 3형식이다.

• Mr. and Mrs. White flew to Russia last summer. …

My wife Harry Mr. and Mrs. White Ken and I Four doctors	drove flew		to	Russia England California New York Miami Beach	last	week. summer. year. weekend. month.
	traveled by	bus ship				
He She They We	took pictures of		snow. mountains. tall buildings. trees and lakes. many different things.		He She They We	went to many
stores. attractions. cities. hotels. diners.	The sky The weather The days The nights		was were	very often sometimes never always	rainy cold hot clear cool sunny	and

the food was	very often sometimes never always	awful. delicious. bad. good.	He She They We	stayed	three days one week one month six weeks
and		wanted to didn't want to			come back. return.

Writing *ex* Four doctors drove to Russia last month. …

1.

2.

3.

4.

5.

164

Rewrite the paragraph. Put in capital letters, apostrophes, commas, quotation marks, question marks and periods, if necessary.

Point

문장의 시작과 끝을 의미로 찾은 후 마침표(period)와 대문자(capital letter)를 활용하여 문장을 다시 구성한다. 그리고 콤마(comma), 아포스트로피(apostrophe), 물음표(question mark), 따옴표(quotation mark), 느낌표(exclamation mark)를 이용하여 문장을 완성한다. 대부분의 문장은 1형식, 2형식 그리고 3형식이다.

steve walked into his office yesterday he looked at his desk his pens pencils and calendar were there but his phone wasnt on his desk wheres my phone then someone said you forgot to pay for your phone this month steve they came and picked it up

Rewriting

165

Number the sentences in the correct time sequence. Then rewrite the sentences as a complete paragraph.

Point

시간순 (time order)을 나타내는 연결사(connectives)들의 의미를 먼저 파악한다. 그리고 주어진 문장을 시간과 논리적 방식에 따라 순서에 맞게 번호를 적은 후 주어진 연결사 중 바른 연결사를 추가하고 생략법과 공통 관계를 이용하여 의미의 일관성(coherence)과 통일성(unity)을 갖춘 완성된 단락(complete paragraph)을 작성한다. 문장은 3형식이다.

CONNECTIVE WORDS THAT INDICATE A TIME SEQUENCE

first/   before that/   in the morning/   after that
second/   eventually/   first[last] of all/   initial(ly)
third/   then/   at the start/   following
fourth/   next/   afterward/   final(ly)

_____ He put the back on the bookcases.
_____ He nailed the shelves in.
_____ He sanded the bookcases.
_____ He measured the wood.
_____ He cut the wood.
_____ He bought materials.

Rewriting

Match the phrases/clauses in column A with those in column B to form sentences. Then rewrite the sentences in order as one paragraph.

Point

column A와 어울리는 표현을 column B에서 찾아 연결한 후 시간순(time order) 그리고 논리순(logical order) 방식에 따라 순서를 정한다. 의미의 일관성(coherence)과 통일성(unity)을 갖춘 완성된 단락(complete paragraph)을 작성한다. 문장은 1형식과 2형식 그리고 3형식이다.

A	B
____ Then he'll go to	a. for a final term exam tomorrow.
____ First, he'll study with	b. study again until 5 o'clock.
____ After lunch he'll	c. relax for about an hour and a half.
____ He thinks this is	d. bed by 10 o'clock.
____ After dinner he'll	e. rest and listen to the music.
____ Then he'll have lunch and	f. Max for three hours.
____ Jack is getting ready	g. a wonderful study schedule.

Rewriting

167

Listen to the paragraph and then read and answer the questions with the help of words and phrases in the boxes. Finally, rewrite a paragraph similar to the one you listened to using the answers.

> **Point**
>
> 먼저 들려주는 지문을 주의깊게 듣는다. 이때 지문 전체의 의미 파악이 중요하다. 다음 박스에 주어진 단어를 활용하여 주어진 질문에 대한 답을 작성한다. 그리고 마지막으로 답을 서로 결합하여 의미의 일관성(coherence)과 문장의 통일성(unity)을 갖춘 지문을 완성하며, 문법적으로 오류가 없도록 유의한다. 듣기 능력(listening ability)과 문법 지식(grammar knowledge)을 배양시키는 학습이다. 문장은 2형식과 3형식이다.

Questions:

1. What is the topic of the paragraph?
2. What is the first thing you can do to increase your chances of living longer?
3. What is the second way to increase your chances of living longer?
4. What can you do to add six months each time you drive?
5. What should you do about your weight to increase your chances for living longer?

1	topic/ how/ increase/ chances/ living longer
2	first/ can do/ not to smoke
3	second way/ exercise/ every day
4	use/ seat belts/ each time/ add six moths
5	finally/ lose/ extra weight

Answers

1.
2.
3.
4.
5.

Rewriting

168

Read the paragraph. Then write the summary of the paragraph with the help of words and phrases in the boxes. (Summaries will vary.)

> **Point**
>
> 먼저 주어진 지문을 주의깊게 읽는다. 그리고 박스 안에 주어진 단어를 사용하여 읽었던 단락을 요약(summary)하여 요약문을 작성한다. 요약문은 2개의 문장으로 완성한다. 문장은 that절을 목적어로 갖는 3형식이다. 단락을 읽을 때는 먼저 의미가 파악되어야 하며, 박스 속에 주어진 단어를 연결하여 문장을 만들 때는 문장의 통일성(unity)에 유의해야 한다. 세련된 문장을 작성하기 위해서 공통 관계와 생략법 등을 최대한 활용하면서 문법을 바르게 적용해야 한다. 또한 콤마(comma)와 물음표(question mark), 마침표(period), 그리고 대문자(capital letter) 등 구두점(punctuation) 사용에 유의한다.

Mr. Goosen needs to get a Florida driver's license. He bought a book to study the traffic laws. He has learned that in Florida people must wear a seat belt at all times and that all children under four years old must be in a safety seat. He also found out that in Florida people must have auto insurance. Mr. Goosen hopes to get his license in a few days after he has learned all about the traffic laws.

1	Goosen/ get/ license
2	has learned/ must/ seat belt/ under/ four/ be in/ safety seat/ people/ insurance

Summary:

Topic:

Main idea:

Read the paragraph. Then write the summary of the paragraph with the help of words and phrases in the boxes. (Summaries will vary.)

> **Point**
>
> 먼저 주어진 지문을 주의깊게 읽는다. 그리고 박스 안에 주어진 단어를 사용하여 읽었던 단락을 요약(summary)하여 요약문을 작성한다. 요약문은 2개의 문장으로 완성한다. 문장은 1형식과 3형식이다. 단락을 읽을 때는 먼저 의미가 파악되어야 하며, 박스 속에 주어진 단어를 연결하여 문장을 만들 때는 문장의 통일성(unity)에 유의해야 한다. 세련된 문장을 작성하기 위해서 공통 관계와 생략법 등을 최대한 활용하면서 문법을 바르게 적용해야 한다. 또한 콤마(comma)와 물음표(question mark), 마침표(period), 그리고 대문자(capital letter) 등 구두점(punctuation) 사용에 유의한다.

For many years, dentists have used gold to repair and fill teeth. They like to use gold because they can shape it easily and use it to fill a tooth. It's soft enough to work with, but it's strong enough to last a long time. Because the price of gold is so high, many of today's dentists are not using as much of it as they did before. More and more, they are using man-made materials instead of gold to repair and fill teeth.

1	used/ repair/ fill/ many years/ because/ easy/ lasted
2	but/ using/ man-made/ instead of / because/ cheaper

Summary:

Topic:

Main idea:

17o

Read the paragraph. Then write the summary of the paragraph with the help of words and phrases in the boxes. (Summaries will vary.)

> **Point**
>
> 먼저 주어진 지문을 주의깊게 읽는다. 그리고 박스 안에 주어진 단어를 사용하여 읽었던 단락을 요약(summary)하여 요약문을 작성한다. 요약문은 3개의 문장으로 완성한다. 문장은 1형식, 2형식 그리고 3형식이다. 단락을 읽을 때는 먼저 의미가 파악되어야 하며, 박스 속에 주어진 단어를 연결하여 문장을 만들 때는 문장의 통일성(unity)에 유의해야 한다. 세련된 문장을 작성하기 위해서 공통 관계와 생략법 등을 최대한 활용하면서 문법을 바르게 적용해야 한다. 또한 콤마(comma)와 물음표(question mark), 마침표(period), 그리고 대문자(capital letter) 등 구두점(punctuation) 사용에 유의한다.

Man needs machines to help him study the things that live and grow in the ocean. There have been several machines made in the past, but man couldn't make a careful study using them. Today we have a better machine to help us study the ocean. It's a vehicle like an automobile, which can move to the places we want to study under water. It has large windows which make it easy to see, and it can stay underwater a long time.

1	needs/ study/ ocean
2	there/ in the past/ but/ today/ have/ better
3	vehicle/ large windows/ that/ move and stay /underwater

Summary: ....

....

....

Topic: ....

Main idea: ....

....

192 • Writing Bible

171

Make a paragraph using the words and phrases in the boxes.
(Answers will vary.)

> **Point**
>
> 박스 안에 주어진 단어를 활용하여 의미에 맞게끔 각각의 문장을 만든다. 핵심은 의미의 일관성(coherence)과 통일성(unity)에 있다. 주어의 일치, 동사와 목적어의 관계성 그리고 단·복수의 선택에 유의하면서 단락(paragraph)을 완성한다. 지문(passage)은 길지만 문장은 1형식과 3형식이다.

• Kevin went to the market. …

Mary Paula My father and I Mr. and Mrs. Bush Kevin		went to		the grocery store. the market. the drugstore.		He We They She
bought	cookies food fish films toothpastes	for	their her our his	dessert. trip. lunch. dinner. cat. teeth.	They It	cost didn't cost
much. a lot.	They We She He	also went to		the library the post office the bank the bookstore	and	mailed cashed bought got
many some a				books. packages. letters. stamps. check.		

Writing *ex* Paula went to the drugstore. She bought toothpaste for her teeth. …

1.

2.

3.

4.

5.

172

Match the phrases/clauses in column A with those in column B to form sentences. Then rewrite the sentences in order as one paragraph.

Point

column A와 어울리는 표현을 column B에서 찾아 연결한 후 시간순(time order) 그리고 논리순(logical order) 방식에 따라 순서를 정한다. 의미의 일관성(coherence)과 통일성(unity)을 갖춘 완성된 단락(complete paragraph)을 작성한다. 문장은 1형식, 2형식 그리고 3형식이다.

A	B
____ Sally and Diane ____ Usually they ____ When they arrive at the airport, ____ They do this because it is cheaper to go sightseeing ____ When they go sightseeing, they learn a lot about ____ This new information about the people and places	a. they rent a car. b. by car than by taxi. c. like to travel. d. travel by plane. e. the people and places. f. is exciting for Sally and Diane.

Rewriting

173

Read the paragraph; then choose a word for each number. Add the words to the paragraph and rewrite it on the lines below. (Answers will vary.)

Point

박스 안에 주어진 단어 중 적절한 단어를 번호에 맞게 선택한 후 주어진 문장에 추가하여 좀 더 길고 완벽한 문장을 만드는 학습이다. 이때 주의해야 할 사항은 의미의 일관성(coherence)이다. 먼저 박스 안에 주어진 단어의 의미가 파악되어야 한다. 문장은 1형식, 2형식 그리고 3형식이다.

People like to shop at a (1). They can park in(on) the (2). There are (3) and many other kinds of stores. There are many places to (4) at while you shop. It's (5) to (6) at a (7).

1. store/ mall/ super market
2. garage/ street/ parking lot
3. clothing stores/ variety stores/ restaurants
4. eat/ exercise/ rest/
5. nice/ crowded/ busy
6. go shopping/ park the car/ eat lunch
7. parking lot/ mall/ cafeteria

Rewriting

174

Read the paragraph. Then write the summary of the paragraph with the help of words and phrases in the boxes. (Summaries will vary.)

Point

먼저 주어진 지문을 주의깊게 읽는다. 그리고 박스 안에 주어진 단어를 사용하여 읽었던 단락을 요약(summary)하여 요약문을 작성한다. 요약문은 3개의 문장으로 완성한다. 문장은 2형식, 3형식 그리고 5형식(help동사의 용법)이다. 단락을 읽을 때는 먼저 의미가 파악되어야 하며, 박스 속에 주어진 단어를 연결하여 문장을 만들 때는 문장의 통일성(unity)에 유의해야 한다. 세련된 문장을 작성하기 위해서 공통 관계와 생략법 등을 최대한 활용하면서 문법을 바르게 적용해야 한다. 또한 콤마(comma)와 물음표(question mark), 마침표(period), 그리고 대문자(capital letter) 등 구두점(punctuation) 사용에 유의한다.

Education is very important, but when you work at a job you often learn more than you do in school. Professionals will tell you they learned more about their profession during their first year at work than in all their years in college. So, while still in college, students should try to work in their field. The experience they get will help them decide if they like the field, and it will help them find jobs later.

1	important/ but/ learn/ at a job/ than/ in school
2	in college/ should/ work/ fields
3	experience/ help/ decide/ if/ like/ help/ find/ later

Summary:

Topic:

Main idea:

175

Read the paragraph. Then write the summary of the paragraph with the help of words and phrases in the boxes. (Summaries will vary.)

> **Point**
>
> 먼저 주어진 지문을 주의깊게 읽는다. 그리고 박스 안에 주어진 단어를 사용하여 읽었던 단락을 요약(summary)하여 요약문을 작성한다. 요약문은 2개의 문장으로 완성한다. 문장은 1형식, 2형식 그리고 3형식이다. 단락을 읽을 때는 먼저 의미가 파악되어야 하며, 박스 속에 주어진 단어를 연결하여 문장을 만들 때는 문장의 통일성(unity)에 유의해야 한다. 세련된 문장을 작성하기 위해서 공통 관계와 생략법 등을 최대한 활용하면서 문법을 바르게 적용해야 한다. 또한 콤마(comma)와 물음표(question mark), 마침표(period), 그리고 대문자(capital letter) 등 구두점(punctuation) 사용에 유의한다.

Polyester is a man-made material. We use it to make many things—from automobile tires to the clothes we wear. It's a very strong material. It lasts a long time and is easy to clean. Polyester and natural materials together make clothes that are easy to wear in all kinds of weather and climates. People in the United States use Polyester and other man-made materials more than natural materials. Polyester is also becoming very popular in other countries.

1	polyester/ man-made/ and/ from/ to
2	strong/ long time/ used/ clothe/ wear

Summary: _____

_____

_____

Topic: _____

Main idea: _____

_____

176

Read the paragraph. Then write the summary of the paragraph with the help of words and phrases in the boxes. (Summaries will vary.)

> **Point**
>
> 먼저 주어진 지문을 주의깊게 읽는다. 그리고 박스 안에 주어진 단어를 사용하여 읽었던 단락을 요약(summary)하여 요약문을 작성한다. 요약문은 3개의 문장으로 완성한다. 문장은 1형식과 3형식이다. 단락을 읽을 때는 먼저 의미가 파악되어야 하며, 박스 속에 주어진 단어를 연결하여 문장을 만들 때는 문장의 통일성(unity)에 유의해야 한다. 세련된 문장을 작성하기 위해서 공통 관계와 생략법 등을 최대한 활용하면서 문법을 바르게 적용해야 한다. 또한 콤마(comma)와 물음표(question mark), 마침표(period), 그리고 대문자(capital letter) 등 구두점(punctuation) 사용에 유의한다.

Samuel Colt was always interested in guns. He thought about them a lot and always looked for new ideas. When he was a sailor on a ship to India, he was watching the wheel on the ship. This gave him an idea for a new kind of gun. He drew pictures of this new kind of gun, but he changed the pictures after he got to India because the things he saw there gave him more new ideas. At first, his ideas didn't work, but Samuel tried again and again until he made a weapon that could repeat shots without reloading. Samuel Colt was able to do that because he liked for new ideas and never stopped trying.

1	Samuel Colt/ interested/ guns
2	got/ ideas/ ship/ India
3	finally/ new/ because/ looked for/ and/ stopped

Summary:

Topic:

Main idea:

177

Rewrite the paragraph. Put in capital letters, apostrophes, commas, quotation marks, question marks, exclamation marks and periods, if necessary.

Point

문장의 시작과 끝을 의미로 찾은 후 마침표(period)와 대문자(capital letter)를 활용하여 문장을 다시 구성한다. 그리고 콤마(comma), 아포스트로피(apostrophe), 물음표(question mark), 따옴표(quotation mark) 그리고 느낌표(exclamation mark)를 이용하여 문장을 완성한다. 대부분의 문장은 1형식, 2형식 그리고 3형식이다.

do you borrow anything from others do you lend anything to others of course you do so do most of us so do western people but in the west there are more principles than in the east you can borrow things from others but you must return them later no matter whether its one dollar or only a pencil moreover you must make sure that the thing is as good as before if you break it you must pay for it do you think they are reasonable

Rewriting

178

Match the phrases/clauses in column A with those in column B to form sentences. Then rewrite the sentences in order as one paragraph.

> **Point**
>
> column A와 어울리는 표현을 column B에서 찾아 연결한 후 시간순(time order) 그리고 논리순(logical order) 방식에 따라 순서를 정한다. 의미의 일관성(coherence)과 통일성(unity)을 갖춘 완성된 단락(complete paragraph)을 작성한다. 문장은 1형식, 3형식 그리고 4형식이다.

A	B
____ At 10:00 he called the	a. headache when he got up.
____ She gave him a	b. about his symptoms.
____ Thursday morning Ted had a	c. 2 o'clock appointment.
____ The woman on the phone asked Ted	d. doctor's office.
____ Ted answered	e. that he had a physical 3 weeks ago.
____ By 9 o'clock he had a cough, a runny	f. the date of his last checkup.
____ Ted sneezed, coughed, and said, "Thanks. See	g. nose, and a temperature.
____ She also asked about	h. you at 2 o'clock."

Rewriting

179

Combine the ideas into some sentences. And then rewrite a paragraph with the new sentences. (Rewritings will vary.)

Point

공통 관계(common relation)와 생략(ellipsis)법을 적용하여 문장을 간소화한다. 먼저 각각의 문장을 읽고 이해한 후 주어와 동사 그리고 목적어의 공통 관계를 파악한다. 그리고 생략법에 따라 문장을 결합한다. 무엇보다 문장의 통일성(unity)에 유의해야 한다. 필요한 경우에 적절한 접속사, 관계 대명사, 전치사, (대)명사, (대)동사, 조동사 그리고 형용사나 부사 등을 사용하여 단락 전체의 의미를 좀 더 명확하게 한다. 그러나 단락의 일관성(coherence)은 유지해야 한다. "/ /" 속에 포함된 문장들을 결합시켜 하나의 문장으로 다시 작성하여 단락을 완성한다. 문장은 2형식과 5형식(let동사의 용법)이다.

/ Mike's appearance is very important in his job. // He is a businessman. People place their trust in him. // He must look neat. He must look responsible. He must look dependable while he is at work. // His job is so demanding. On weekends, he relaxes. // He lets his beard grow. He wears old clothes. // He doesn't look like the same man everyone trusts and depends on at work. /

Rewriting

18o

Listen to the paragraph and then read and answer the questions with the help of words and phrases in the boxes. Finally, rewrite a paragraph similar to the one you listened to using the answers.

> **Point**
>
> 먼저 들려주는 지문을 주의깊게 듣는다. 이때 지문 전체의 의미 파악이 중요하다. 다음 박스에 주어진 단어를 활용하여 주어진 질문에 대한 답을 작성한다. 그리고 마지막으로 답을 서로 결합하여 의미의 일관성(coherence)과 문장의 통일성(unity)을 갖춘 지문을 완성하며, 문법적으로 오류가 없도록 유의한다. 듣기 능력(listening ability)과 문법 지식(grammar knowledge)을 배양시키는 학습이다. 문장은 2형식과 3형식이다.

Questions:

1. What was an important year for the U.S.?
2. Why was it an important year?
3. What else happened in 1976?
4. How many women started at the academies?
5. What year won't the people forget?

1	the year 1976/ important/ United States
2	200th birthday/ country
3	also/ that year/ women/ entered/ U S. military academies
4	355/ women/ attended/ academies
5	year/ American women/ men/ forget

Answers

1.
2.
3.
4.
5.

Rewriting

181

Read the paragraph. Then write the summary of the paragraph with the help of words and phrases in the boxes. (Summaries will vary.)

Point

먼저 주어진 지문을 주의깊게 읽는다. 그리고 박스 안에 주어진 단어를 사용하여 읽었던 단락을 요약(summary)하여 요약문을 작성한다. 요약문은 3개의 문장으로 완성한다. 문장은 3행식이다. 단락을 읽을 때는 먼저 의미가 파악되어야 하며, 박스 속에 주어진 단어를 연결하여 문장을 만들 때는 문장의 통일성(unity)에 유의해야 한다. 세련된 문장을 작성하기 위해서 공통 관계와 생략법 등을 최대한 활용하면서 문법을 바르게 적용해야 한다. 또한 콤마(comma)와 물음표(question mark), 마침표(period), 그리고 대문자(capital letter) 등 구두점(punctuation) 사용에 유의한다.

Did you put some coins in a machine to buy gum or a can of soda today? Then you used a vending machine. People began to use vending machines in the United States in the 1890s, and could buy gum, stamps, and peanuts from these machines at train stations. Then in the 1900s, people could buy drinks and other foods from vending machines. Today, vending machines can sell some unusual things such as toys and stockings, and some machines can even talk.

1	people/ using/ in the 1890s
2	sold/ gum/ peanuts
3	today/ unusual/ some/ talk

Summary:

Topic:

Main idea:

182

Read the paragraph. Then write the summary of the paragraph with the help of words and phrases in the boxes. (Summaries will vary.)

> **Point**
>
> 먼저 주어진 지문을 주의깊게 읽는다. 그리고 박스 안에 주어진 단어를 사용하여 읽었던 단락을 요약(summary)하여 요약문을 작성한다. 요약문은 3개의 문장으로 완성한다. 문장은 2형식과 3형식이다. 단락을 읽을 때는 먼저 의미가 파악되어야 하며, 박스 속에 주어진 단어를 연결하여 문장을 만들 때는 문장의 통일성(unity)에 유의해야 한다. 세련된 문장을 작성하기 위해서 공통 관계와 생략법 등을 최대한 활용하면서 문법을 바르게 적용해야 한다. 또한 콤마(comma)와 물음표(question mark), 마침표(period), 그리고 대문자(capital letter) 등 구두점(punctuation) 사용에 유의한다.

Your home is one of the most dangerous places in the world. Every year hundreds of people have accidents in their homes. Many people fall down stairs or slip on wet floors in their bathrooms. Careless people leave cigarettes that cause fires and burn homes and apartments. Grease fires that start on stoves in kitchens also cause terrible fires. Many times parents let children play in the kitchen while the mother is cooking. Sometimes hot food spills on the child, or the child cuts his hands with a knife. Accidents like this shouldn't happen. People need to be careful in their homes. They need to practice being safe all the time.

1	home/ dangerous
2	careless/ cause/ many/ in/ homes
3	need/ careful/ practice/ safe/ homes

Summary: ....

....

....

Topic:

Main idea:

183

Read the paragraph. Then write the summary of the paragraph with the help of words and phrases in the boxes. (Summaries will vary.)

> **Point**
>
> 먼저 주어진 지문을 주의깊게 읽는다. 그리고 박스 안에 주어진 단어를 사용하여 읽었던 단락을 요약(summary)하여 요약문을 작성한다. 요약문은 3개의 문장으로 완성한다. 문장은 2형식과 3형식이다. 단락을 읽을 때는 먼저 의미가 파악되어야 하며, 박스 속에 주어진 단어를 연결하여 문장을 만들 때는 문장의 통일성(unity)에 유의해야 한다. 세련된 문장을 작성하기 위해서 공통 관계와 생략법 등을 최대한 활용하면서 문법을 바르게 적용해야 한다. 또한 콤마(comma)와 물음표(question mark), 마침표(period), 그리고 대문자(capital letter) 등 구두점(punctuation) 사용에 유의한다.

Some English words come other languages. For example, the word "gun" comes from a Norwegian word "Gunnhildr." This word came from a woman's name, Dame Gunidda, who lived in the country of Norway about 670 years ago. The word "rifle" is the German word. In the United States, German gun makers made the first rifles in Pennsylvania about 1776. These are just two examples of how English uses words from other languages.

1	some/ words/ from/ other
2	gun/ from/ Norwegian
3	rifle/ comes/ German

Summary:

Topic:

Main idea:

184

Make a perfect paragraph using the words in the boxes. (Answers will vary.)

> **Point**
>
> 박스 안에 주어진 단어를 활용하여 의미에 맞게끔 각각의 문장을 만든다. 핵심은 의미의 일관성(coherence)과 통일성(unity)에 있다. 주어의 일치, 동사와 목적어의 관계성, 부사(구)와 부사(구) 간의 관계성 그리고 등위 접속사 and와 but의 선택에 유의하면서 단락(paragraph)을 완성한다. 지문(passage)은 길지만 문장은 1형식, 2형식 그리고 3형식이다.

• I wanted to eat breakfast at a small restaurant this morning. …

Mr. and Mrs. Brown Alicia My uncle I My nephew	wanted to eat	breakfast lunch a snack dinner	at a	good new crowded small
cafeteria diner restaurant snack bar	this evening. last night. this morning. yesterday.	She They He I	sat at a table stood in line	for
twenty minutes. a long time. a few minutes. only a minute.	The waiter The waitress	was very	slow, fast, nice, young,	and but
the food cost	a lot of only a little	money.	They She He I	stayed there went home.
and ate a good meal.				

208 • Writing Bible

Writing

ex Alice wanted to eat a snack at a good snack bar yesterday. She sat at a table for a long time...

1.

2.

3.

4.

5.

185

Rewrite the paragraph. Put in capital letters, apostrophes, commas and periods, if necessary.

Point

문장의 시작과 끝을 의미로 찾은 후 마침표(period)와 대문자(capital letter)를 활용하여 문장을 다시 구성한다. 그리고 콤마(comma), 아포스트로피(apostrophe), 물음표(question mark), 따옴표(quotation mark) 그리고 느낌표(exclamation mark) 등을 이용하여 바른 문장을 완성한다. 대부분의 문장은 1형식, 2형식 그리고 3형식이다.

---

thanksgiving day is a holiday in the usa it is on the fourth thursday of november on that day families and friends get together for a turkey dinner people leave work early on wednesday afternoon and drive their cars to distant places for a family reunion there was a story about thanksgiving day when the first english settlers arrived in america in 1621 they didnt have enough food with the indians help they had a good harvest the english invited the indians to their dinner in order to give thanks to them for their help and to god

Rewriting

186

Read the paragraph. Change it from the present tense to the past tense. Underline the words that need to be changed; then rewrite the paragraph with the changes.

Point

현재시제(present tense)를 과거시제(past tense)로 바꿔 각각의 문장을 다시 작성한다. 먼저 전환이 필요한 단어에 밑줄을 긋는다. 가능한 경우 현재시제를 미래시제(future tense)로 전환시켜 다양한 형태의 문장을 학습한다. 문장은 1형식, 3형식 그리고 5형식(help동사의 용법)이다.

When Sony visits his uncle in St. Louis, he does the same things every day. First, he eats a big breakfast. Then, he helps his uncle clean up the house. After that, they take a trip to the gym for a two-hour workout. In the afternoon, they take a one-hour nap, and then they play cards until it's time for dinner. After dinner, they take a three-mile walk. When they get home, it's time for a shower and bed. Sony is in real good shape when he gets home from his uncle's house.

Rewriting

187

Number the sentences in the correct time sequence. Then rewrite the sentences as a complete paragraph.

Point

시간순(time order)을 나타내는 연결사(connectives)들의 의미를 먼저 파악한다. 그리고 주어진 문장을 시간과 논리적 방식에 따라 순서에 맞게 번호를 적은 후 주어진 연결사 중 바른 연결사를 추가하여 의미의 일관성(coherence)과 통일성(unity)을 갖춘 완성된 단락(complete paragraph)을 작성한다. 문장은 3형식과 5형식(help동사의 용법)이다.

CONNECTIVE WORDS THAT INDICATE A TIME SEQUENCE

first/   before that/   in the morning/   after that
second/   eventually/   first[last] of all/   initial(ly)
third/   then/   at the start/   following
fourth/   next/   after/   final(ly)

_____ Judy helped him measure the wood.
_____ She held the wood.
_____ Tom sawed it.
_____ Judy helped Tom build new bookcases.
_____ They had lunch.
_____ Judy took the kids to the swimming pool.

Rewriting

188

Match the phrases/clauses in column A with those in column B to form sentences. Then rewrite the sentences in order as one paragraph.

Point

column A와 어울리는 표현을 column B에서 찾아 연결한 후 시간순(time order) 그리고 논리순(logical order) 방식에 따라 순서를 정한다. 의미의 일관성(coherence)과 통일성(unity)을 갖춘 완성된 단락(complete paragraph)을 작성한다. 문장은 2형식과 3형식이다.

A	B
___ Mark is having a dinner	a. of tomatoes and onions.
___ He always uses carrots	b. with cheese.
___ First, he'll serve a cream soup	c. party this evening.
___ Finally, for dessert he'll	d. but Mark likes dinner parties.
___ Then for the meat dish, he'll	e. when he makes his dish.
___ Second, he'll serve a salad	f. serve fruit and ice cream.
___ That kind of meal is a lot of work,	g. serve chicken and vegetables.

Rewriting

189

Read the paragraph; then choose a word for each number. Add the words to the paragraph and rewrite it on the lines below. (Answers will vary.)

Point

박스 안에 주어진 단어 중 적절한 단어를 번호에 맞게 선택한 후 주어진 문장에 추가하여 좀 더 길고 완벽한 문장을 만드는 학습이다. 이때 주의해야 할 사항은 의미의 일관성(coherence)이다. 먼저 박스 안에 주어진 단어의 의미가 파악되어야 한다. 문장은 1형식, 2형식 그리고 3형식이다.

A (1) boy (2) walked across a (3) street. At the same time, a (4) car was traveling in (5) direction. (6), the child didn't see the car. But the man in the car was a (7) driver, and he saw the child (8). He stopped (9) car, got out, and picked up the (10) child. Then he took him home.

1. tired/ little/ young/ smart
2. carelessly/ slowly/ carefully/ fast
3. wide/ busy/ quite/ narrow
4. big/ fast/ red/ white
5. the boy's/ his/ the child's/ the man's
6. Because he was tired/ Because he forgot to look
7. good/ careful/ terrific/ terrible
8. right away/ in time
9. the/ his
10. tired/ small/ heavy/ dull

Rewriting

19o

Combine the ideas into some sentences. And then rewrite a paragraph with the new sentences. (Rewritings will vary.)

Point

공통 관계(common relation)와 생략(ellipsis)법을 적용하여 문장을 간소화한다. 먼저 각각의 문장을 읽고 이해한 후 주어와 동사 그리고 목적어의 공통 관계를 파악한다. 그리고 생략법에 따라 문장을 결합한다. 무엇보다 문장의 통일성(unity)에 유의해야 한다. 필요한 경우에 적절한 접속사, 관계 대명사, 전치사, (대)명사, (대)동사, 조동사 그리고 형용사나 부사 등을 사용하여 단락 전체의 의미를 좀 더 명확하게 한다. 그러나 단락의 일관성(coherence)은 유지해야 한다. "/ /" 속에 포함된 문장들을 결합시켜 하나의 문장으로 다시 작성하여 단락을 완성한다. 문장은 2형식, 3형식, 4형식(tell동사의 용법) 그리고 5형식(make동사의 용법)이다.

/ Mr. White fell asleep. He was on duty. It was only 10 a.m. He had slept very little the night before. // He had taken some pills. The pills were for losing weight. They had made him very nervous. The pills also kept him awake all night. // A friend had recommended the pills. The friend didn't say anything about being nervous. The friend didn't say anything about staying awake all night. // Mr. White learned something. He learned to be careful about medication. He learned to check it out with a doctor before taking it. /

Rewriting

191

Read the paragraph. Then write the summary of the paragraph with the help of words and phrases in the boxes. (Summaries will vary.)

> **Point**
>
> 먼저 주어진 지문을 주의깊게 읽는다. 그리고 박스 안에 주어진 단어를 사용하여 읽었던 단락을 요약(summary)하여 요약문을 작성한다. 요약문은 3개의 문장으로 완성한다. 문장은 2형식과 3형식이다. 단락을 읽을 때는 먼저 의미가 파악되어야 하며, 박스 속에 주어진 단어를 연결하여 문장을 만들 때는 문장의 통일성(unity)에 유의해야 한다. 세련된 문장을 작성하기 위해서 공통 관계와 생략법 등을 최대한 활용하면서 문법을 바르게 적용해야 한다. 또한 콤마(comma)와 물음표(question mark), 마침표(period), 그리고 대문자(capital letter) 등 구두점(punctuation) 사용에 유의한다.

The Astrodome is a large sports stadium in Houston, Texas. It opened in 1965. It was the first stadium with a cover or "dome," so people could use it in all kinds of weather. The stadium has room for 66,000 people. The floor is man-made grass which doesn't grow, so it doesn't need watering or cutting. The stadium's name is "astrodome" because Houston is also the home of the United States astronauts—the men and women who travel in space.

1	Astrodome/ Houston, Texas/ stadium/ cover
2	room/ people/ and/ floor/ man-made /grass
3	it/ because/ in the city/ that/ home/ astronauts

Summary:

Topic:

Main idea:

192

Read the paragraph. Then write the summary of the paragraph with the help of words and phrases in the boxes. (Summaries will vary.)

> **Point**
>
> 먼저 주어진 지문을 주의깊게 읽는다. 그리고 박스 안에 주어진 단어를 사용하여 읽었던 단락을 요약(summary)하여 요약문을 작성한다. 요약문은 3개의 문장으로 완성한다. 문장은 1형식, 2형식 그리고 3형식이다. 단락을 읽을 때는 먼저 의미가 파악되어야 하며, 박스 속에 주어진 단어를 연결하여 문장을 만들 때는 문장의 통일성(unity)에 유의해야 한다. 세련된 문장을 작성하기 위해서 공통 관계와 생략법 등을 최대한 활용하면서 문법을 바르게 적용해야 한다. 또한 콤마(comma)와 물음표(question mark), 마침표(period), 그리고 대문자(capital letter) 등 구두점(punctuation) 사용에 유의한다.

There are many kinds of grasses. In fact, there are more than 4,700 different kinds of grasses. Grass can grow as tall as a man. There are many grasses like corn and rice that we do not usually think of as grasses, but they are. Both man and animals eat these grasses. Grass is not only important as a food; it is also important to the land during heavy rains. Grass keeps the land from becoming a desert. Certain animals kill grass because when they eat it, they cut it too close to the ground. When this happens and there is no grass, a heavy rain will take the dirt away, or a strong wind will blow the dirt away. Some deserts of the world once had grass thousands of years ago. Someday, these places might have a "green carpet" again.

1	there/ kinds/ grasses
2	man/ animals/ eat/ some of
3	also/ important/ keep/ from/ desert

Summary:

Topic:

Main idea:

Read the paragraph. Then write the summary of the paragraph with the help of words and phrases in the boxes. (Summaries will vary.)

> **Point**
>
> 먼저 주어진 지문을 주의깊게 읽는다. 그리고 박스 안에 주어진 단어를 사용하여 읽었던 단락을 요약(summary) 하여 요약문을 작성한다. 요약문은 4개의 문장으로 완성한다. 문장은 1형식이다. 단락을 읽을 때는 먼저 의미가 파악되어야 하며, 박스 속에 주어진 단어를 연결하여 문장을 만들 때는 문장의 통일성(unity)에 유의해야 한다. 세련된 문장을 작성하기 위해서 공통 관계와 생략법 등을 최대한 활용하면서 문법을 바르게 적용해야 한다. 또한 콤마(comma)와 물음표(question mark), 마침표(period), 그리고 대문자(capital letter) 등 구두점 (punctuation) 사용에 유의한다.

Do you know how a traffic signal light works? On some lights, a clock inside the box keeps the signal changing regularly. Other signal lights do not use clocks. They use a wire that goes under the street. Cars and trucks going over the wire make the light change. A third kind of signal light has a button that people push to change the light when they want to cross the intersection.

1	traffic/ work/ different
2	kind/ clocks
3	another/ wires/ streets
4	third/ works with/ buttons/ push

Summary:

Topic:

Main idea:

Read the paragraph. Then write the summary of the paragraph with the help of words and phrases in the boxes. (Summaries will vary.)

> **Point**
>
> 먼저 주어진 지문을 주의깊게 읽는다. 그리고 박스 안에 주어진 단어를 사용하여 읽었던 단락을 요약(summary)하여 요약문을 작성한다. 요약문은 5개의 문장으로 완성한다. 문장은 1형식, 2형식 그리고 3형식이다. 단락을 읽을 때는 먼저 의미가 파악되어야 하며, 박스 속에 주어진 단어를 연결하여 문장을 만들 때는 문장의 통일성(unity)에 유의해야 한다. 세련된 문장을 작성하기 위해서 공통 관계와 생략법 등을 최대한 활용하면서 문법을 바르게 적용해야 한다. 또한 콤마(comma)와 물음표(question mark), 마침표(period), 그리고 대문자(capital letter) 등 구두점(punctuation) 사용에 유의한다.

Andy was tired of studying. He took off his eye-glasses, put down his coffee cup, and closed his eyes. He had been reading for two hours. He got up from his chair and raised his arms over his head. He looked out the window and saw a little boy and girl walking with their mother. He remembered his own family. A few minutes later, he looked at the clock, sat down, and began to study again.

1	Andy/ had/ studying/ hours
2	tired
3	got up/ desk/ looked out
4	some people/ reminded/ family
5	later/ again

Summary:

Topic:

Main idea:

Part IV

Exercise

195

Making a Story. Make your own story using given instructions. [Answers will vary.]

Instructions

1. the material it's made of
2. the colors of the material
3. what we use it for

Writing

Making a story [Inference - Past tense]

Read the information. Then make a story with given words. [Answers will vary.]

Information

Frank felt sick, and he was afraid he couldn't go to dinner.

1	warm/ class
2	head/ stomach
3	keep on/ lesson
4	worry/ invitation

Writing

Making a story [Inference - Past tense]

Read the information. Then make a story with given words. [Answers will vary.]

Information

Tina was in a museum. She was looking at hunting and fishing equipments.

1	items/ hundreds of
2	see/ clothes
3	dishes/ cooking and eating
4	history/ interesting

Writing

Making a Story [Inference - Past or Future tense]

Read the information. Then make a story with given words and phrases.
[Answers will vary.]

Information

Mary is poor and hopes to get money for cleaning the apartments.

1	broom/ mop/ scrub/ brush/ windows
2	many/ building
3	hard work/ buy/ week

Writing

Making a story [Inference - Past tense]

Read the information. Then make a story with given words and phrases.
[Answers will vary.]

Information

Jenifer was expecting her guests.

1	slice/ strawberries/ bowl
2	sugar/ cream
3	put/ cake
4	dessert/ in time/ doorbell

Writing

Making a story [Inference - Past tense]

Read the information. Then make a story with given words and phrases.
[Answers will vary.]

Information

The coach believed that Tina had an injury.

1	tennis/ twist
2	take out of
3	angry/ stop playing

Writing

Making a story [Inference - Past tense and Present Progressive]

Read the information. Then make a story with given words. [Answers will vary.]

Information

Frank and Patty are tourists.

1	stand/ downtown
2	camera/ neck/ map
3	wear

Writing

Making a story [Inference - Past tense]

Read the information. Then make a story with given words. [Answers will vary.]

Information

Mark and Ellen had good seats.

1	concert
2	locate/ middle
3	orchestra
4	parts/ stage
5	glad/ seats

Writing

Making a story [Inference - Past tense]

Read the information. Then make a story with given words. [Answers will vary.]

Information

Alice would rather not see another musical.

1	musical/ first time
2	story/ not/ actor/ actress
3	like/ dancing
4	music/ unnecessary

Writing

Making a story [Inference - Present and Past tense]

First, look at the chart. Then make a story with the information using given words and phrases. [Answers will vary.]

Information

Jane started English class four weeks ago.

grade \ week	week 1	week 2	week 3	week 4
Poor	L / S	S		
Good		L	L / S	S
Very good				L

S: Speaking L: Listening

1	Jane/ start/ class/ ago
2	end/ first week/ listening/ also
3	study/ words/ understand/ a little better
4	second week/ good/ still
5	third week/ also
6	fourth week/ but/ only
7	know/ need

Writing

Making a story [Inference - Past tense]

First, look at the chart. Then make a story with the information using given words and phrases. [Answers will vary.]

Information

Alex must be careful about how much money he spends.

DETAILS / DAYS	HAD	RECEIVED	SPENT
Monday	$50.00		$5.00
Tuesday		$10.00	
Wednesday		$45.00	
Thursday			$20.00
Friday			
Saturday			$10.00

1	Alex/ only/ wallet/ whole week
2	lunch/ newspaper/ $5.00
3	next/ meet/ owe
4	glad/ get back
5	return/ clothing store/ refund
6	evening/ dinner
7	laundry bill

Writing

Making a story [Inference - Present Tense or Future Tense]

Look at Mr. Howard's Schedule. Then make a story with his plans using given words. [Answers will vary.]

Information

The two weeks of this month are going to be very busy weeks for Mr. Howard.

OCTOBER							REMARKS
SUN	MON	TUES	WED	THUR	FRI	SAT	
				1	2	3	
4 dinner	5	6 library car	7 lunch	8	9 wedding	10	
11	12	13 physical	14 test	15 vacation	16	17	

1	wife
2	return/ buy
3	meet
4	has to/ 6 p.m.
5	clinic/ annual
6	driver's license
7	begin/ two weeks

Writing

PART IV • 233

Making a story [Inference - Past tense]

Read the information. Then make a story with given words and phrases.
[Answers will vary.]

Information

Scott was going to a foreign country. He was in the office to get a visa.

1	application/ visa
2	documents/ watch
3	as soon as/ behind the desk

Writing

208

Making a story [Inference - future tense]

Read the information. Then make a story with the given words. [Answers will vary.]

Information

Mark and Paula will need a large room for the reception.

1	get married
2	invite/ wedding
3	barbecue/ guest
4	cake/ drink
5	meal/ dance

Writing

Making a story [Inference - Past tense]

Read the information. Then make a story with the given words. [Answers will vary.]

Information

Mr. and Mrs. Brown were travelling by air.

1	see/ snow/ mountain tops
2	river/ like/ strips/ below
3	valleys/ looked/ ground/ now/ narrow
4	clouds/ close/ touch

Writing

210

Making a story [Inference - Past progressive tense]

Read the information. Then make a story with the given words. [Answers will vary.]

Information

Students were having a barbecue.

1	some/ sitting/ ground/ hamburgers/ salad
2	picnic table/ other/ helping/ putting/ catsup/ plates
3	somewhere/ smell/ wood/ burning

Writing

Sample Answers

Sample Answers

001
1. Open your notebook.
2. Don't circle the number.
3. Listen to music.
4. Never say a word.
5. Write your name.

002
1. This is my dictionary.
2. That is a number.
3. It is a letter.
4. This is his watch.
5. That is her picture.

003
1. I am not a cook.
2. You are a musician.
3. He is an artist.
4. She is not a babysitter.
5. Jane is a doctor.

004
1. Yes, I'm a nurse.
2. No, you're not a policeman.
3. Yes, she is an actress.
4. No, Paula is not a model.
5. Yes, Mark is an editor.

005
1. The pillows are in the bedroom.
2. Your key is not under the table.
3. His bicycle is in the house.
4. Our pictures are on the wall.
5. The book is not in the box.

006
1. Fred is very sick.
2. Ms. Creamer isn't satisfied.
3. The students are very cold.
4. He is very scared.
5. Kathy is relieved.

007
Do you like to walk? I do. It's good for you. All you need is good shoes. Take a friend with you. You can talk and walk at the same time. Walk together every day. You'll feel good.

008
2-4-1-3-5

Please tell me how to operate this machine.
Put your money in the slot.
Push the button.
Get it out.
Get the exact change.

009
2-1-3

Yesterday, Tim wanted to make a long distance call.
He got some change and went to the pay phone.
He dialed the number, but the line was busy.

010
They were happy to see each other after several years. They were pleased.

011
1. The lawyer is lonely. He is in his house.
2. The reporter is in love. She is in the swimming pool.
3. The models are hurt. They are in the clinic.
4. The florists are happy. They are in the cafeteria.
5. The players are excited. They are in the gymnasium.

12

1. The couriers eat chicken burgers for their snack.
2. The clerks eat beef for dinner.
3. The announcer eats a cheese sandwich for every meal.
4. The travel agents eat toasts for lunch.
5. The babysitter eats fruit for breakfast.

13

Frank, Robert, and Joe wanted to take a vacation together. Frank and Joe wanted to go to the mountains, but Robert wanted to go to the lake. Frank said, "Why do we always have to go to the lake? Let's go to the mountains this year!"

14

4-3-1-2

Mark and Karen are in the same Spanish class.

Mark said, "Karen, let's study for the test together."

Karen said, "Okay, Mark. Your house or mine?"

Mark said, "At your house, Karen. We studied for the last test at mine."

15

3-2-1-4

Mike is upset because the airline lost his baggage.

They apologized for losing the baggage.

They hope to find it by tomorrow.

He's worried that they won't find it at all.

16

Marty was very angry when the vending machine was out of order.

17

Summary
Speed, not size, is the thing that's most important to a soccer player.

Topic
A Physical Feature of a Soccer Player

Main idea
Speed, not other physical shapes, is the most important thing to a soccer player.

18

Summary
Keith always makes a good grade on a test because she knows how to study for it.

Topic
Keith's How to Study for a Test

Main idea
Keith knows the way to study for a test, so she does a good job on a test.

19

Summary
The old man who got on the crowded bus didn't have to stand up because a polite young man gave him a seat.

20

1. Where is my book?
2. Where are my glasses?
3. Where is the pay phone?
4. Where is the cafeteria?
5. Where is Bill?

21

1. Whose jacket is this?
2. Whose friends are they?
3. Whose television is that?
4. Whose pants are these?
5. Whose guitars are those?

1. This is my jacket.
2. They are my friends.
3. That's his television.
4. Those are her pants.
5. These are our guitars.

22

Linda watched TV for two hours. Next she took a long shower. She washed her hair. She dried her body and hair with a clean towel. Then a friend called Linda was on the phone. They will have a Korean test tomorrow. Linda didn't study for the test.

o23

He thought the music program on Friday was entertaining and interesting. He enjoyed it very much and many of his friends also thought it was good. There was a good variety of music. He was really glad when his friends invited him to go with them.

o24

3-2-1-4

Mark and Ned visited Mark's mother at his sister's house.

After their visit, Ned said, "I like your mother's house."

Mark said, "Oh, that house isn't hers. It belongs to my sister and her husband."

"Well then," Ned said, "Your sister has a very nice house."

o25

4-2-3-1

Angela cleans rooms in the motel on Maple Street.

She cleans the bedrooms and washes the bathrooms.

She changes the towels, soap and a few other things.

She is a little tired at the end of the day.

o26

The beautiful woman met the handsome sailor at a quiet restaurant.

o27

Summary
Brad reads and collects magazines. He can always find the one he wants in his collection because of the way he keeps them.

Topic
Brad's Magazines

Main idea
Brad reads and collects magazines in his own way.

o28

1. What am I doing?
2. What are you doing?
3. What is Janet doing?
4. What are they doing?
5. What are the children doing?

o29

4-2-3-1

Chris checked in at an old motel.
There were no hangers in the closet.
He couldn't hang up his clothes.
Chris was very angry.

o30

Paula hurt her leg at a soccer game. She didn't go to the doctor. That day her leg was very sore. She went to bed and took medicine. The next day her leg was very sore again. She then went to the doctor's office. Her leg is well now.

o31

Summary
Luke couldn't do his laundry because he didn't have any detergent. The vending machine was out of order, too.

Topic
Luke's Laundry.

Main
The vending machine for detergent is out of order, so Luke didn't do his laundry.

o32

Mr. Black works in an office and keys data into a computer. He prints the information and makes copies of it for his boss, Mr. Green.

o33

The tall woman picked up the heavy box and put it in her red car.

034

4-2-3-1

Last week, Mary went to the bank and opened a checking account.

Today, she got her checks in the mail.

Now she doesn't need to take money with her.

She'll just write a check.

035

I was really excited. I had a ticket for the last baseball game of the year. I was sure it was going to be great! Both teams were strong. I expected to see a lot of people at the stadium. I was not worried because I had reservations and I knew I had a good ticket.

036

3-1-4-2

Henry called the travel agency and made a reservation last week.

Yesterday he went there and picked up his ticket.

Today he must pack his suitcases.

After he packs, he'll be ready for his vacation.

037

The young hostess cut the apple pie and put it on the clean plate.

038

Susan became frightened when the bald, elderly man in the park sat down beside her and started to speak. He had a dishonest face and she didn't trust him.

039

Summary

Janet is a good businesswoman who works for a magazine. She has to work hard at her job because she wants to keep it.

040

Summary

Large pieces of ice cover parts of the world when the weather stays cold for a long time. This ice can change the land and the way it looks.

Topic

Large Pieces of Ice

Main idea

Large pieces of ice can change the land according to movement.

041

Every morning, Susan eats a big breakfast. She eats two eggs, one slice of bread and a banana. She drinks a glass of carrot juice and a big cup of tea. Susan says she is ready to go to work after a good breakfast.

042

Mr. Brown rented a big apartment with a blue couch and a big bookcase.

043

1-4-3-2-5

Jane and Sara went to the gym.

They played a game of table-tennis there.

After the game, Jane said, "I'm hot!"

Sara said, "Let's take a shower."

After their showers, they went to the cafeteria near the gym.

044

3-2-1-4

Yesterday, Ben had a car accident.

He was stopping for a red light, and the car behind him hit him.

Ben wasn't at fault, so the other driver got a ticket.

And the policeman told him to be more careful next time.

045

Working in an office these days is very different from a few years ago. Today, secretaries use computers. They key data into the computer and print out copies when they need them. It's easier to be a secretary now.

046

Summary
Jazz began in New Orleans, Louisiana, in the 1920s. It is just as popular today as it was then. Sometimes people wait in line to hear it.

Topic
Jazz in New Orleans

Main idea
Jazz in New Orleans has been popular to people.

047

4-2-3-1

My brother is a doctor.
He went to school in Los Angeles.
Now he lives in Orange County.
I will visit him next winter.

048

Sarah wanted some drinkables from the vending machine. First, she got some change. Next, she put the money in the slot. After that, she pushed the button under her selection. Then she got her drinkables.

049

Summary
Susan puts shoes on horses. Today she put shoes on Mr. Green's horse, Silver. Silver was nervous at first, but Susan made him calm before she put the shoes on the horse.

Topic
Susan's Interesting Job

Main idea
Susan has an interesting job with a horse, Silver. She really likes her work.

050

The rich man stopped at the new motel to sleep in a clean room.

051

Andy goes to class at 7:30. He listens to the teacher. The teacher sometimes writes on the chalkboard. Andy looks at the chalkboard. The teacher asks a question. Andy can't answer the question. He must study his lesson.

052

1. Linda is watching TV. She is not studying in her room.
2. His brother is reading a newspaper. He is not reading a book in the kitchen.
3. Your dog is eating food. It is not sleeping inside the garden.
4. Eric is going to the gym. He is not going to the library.
5. Her sister is talking to her friend. She is not talking to her mother.

053

4-2-3-1-5

My nephew needs some money.
He lives in New York.
I'll have to mail him the money.
I have to buy a money order.
I'll mail it to him tomorrow afternoon.

054

3-2-4-1-5

Anica was driving her car yesterday.
A policeman stopped her.
He said, "May I see your driver's license?"
Then she said, "I don't have one."
He gave her a ticket.

055

John gets up at 6:30. He takes a shower and shaves. He puts on his clothes. He goes to the cafeteria. He sits down at the table and eats breakfast. Mark sits with John. Mark drinks a cup of coffee. John doesn't drink a cup of coffee in the morning. At 7:15 they walk to class.

056

That old man didn't realize that he spilled coffee on the dirty carpet in his son's old house.

057

A computer has a keyboard, a monitor, and a printer. You use the keyboard to put the data into the computer and the printer to get it out.

058

Tom likes to travel. On his vacation last year he was able to go to London. While he was there he was able to fly to Ireland. He rented a car and was able to drive across Ireland from the east to the west. He wasn't able to get to Paris, but maybe this year he'll be able to go to Europe again.

059

Larry will be studying for an important Korean test tomorrow morning. He will be going to the library in the evening and will be staying there until ten o'clock. He will be reviewing his notes and will be reading the lessons in his book. His friend Ben will be going with him and will be giving him a ride home.

060

2-7-3-1-6-5-4

How do you use this machine?

First, put the money in the slot.

Then make your selection.

Push the button.

Then wait until the snack drops.

Lift the door.

Get it out.

061

2-3-1-4

I got some new things for my apartment.

First, for my living room, I bought a new carpet and a coffee table.

Then for my kitchen, I bought a new oven and blender.

All these things were reasonable, so now I enjoy my apartment more.

062

Summary

Eric is a diplomat. His family travels with him around the world. They enjoy traveling and meeting people.

Topic

Eric who is a diplomat

Main idea

Eric and his family travel around the world and meet people.

063

Script

People have used wheels for quite a long time. The earliest use of the wheel was more than 5,000 years ago in Sumer. The Assyrians began to use wheels about 500 years later. The people in Europe began to use them more than 3,000 years ago.

Title

The Wheels

Rewrite

People have used wheels for a long time. The earliest use of wheels was 5,000 years ago in Sumer. The Assyrians used wheels 500 years later. People in Europe used wheels more than 3,000 years ago.

064

1. What do they do in the morning?
2. Where does Mark eat lunch?
3. What time does Jane go every night?
4. Does Wendy study every morning?
5. How often do you swim?

065

1. Who is talking to my father?
2. Who is drinking orange juice?
3. Who are listening to the tapes?
4. Who are going to the snack bar?
5. Who is reading a book in the park?

1. Eddy is talking to my father.
2. Mr. Casey is drinking orange juice.
3. Sam and Pat are listening to the tapes.
4. My kids are going to the snack bar.

Sample Answers • 245

5. Beth is reading a book in the park.

066

1. Bob never listens to his mother.
2. I hardly sleep in the classroom.
3. Anita often watches TV.
4. The students always study late.
5. The players usually play on Wednesdays.

067

Larry took a trip to New York last month. The weather wasn't very good. It was cold and rainy. Larry didn't have his coat. He was very upset. What did Larry do? He bought a nice brown coat. Larry was in New York for one week. It was a good trip.

068

5-3-1-4-2

At six o'clock, John was hungry.

He went to a little restaurant near his house.

He sat down and looked at the menu.

Then he ordered a big dinner.

After a short time, the waiter brought his food.

069

2-4-1-3

A: Where is Meg?

B: He could be in the dormitory. I saw him there a few minutes ago.

A: I've already checked there. Where else could he be?

B: Well, then he may be at the library. He has a test tomorrow.

A: Which one? The city or school library?

B: I'm not sure. He uses both.

A: Thanks. I'll try the city library.

B: Good luck!

070

Susan is a happy girl because she made a high score on her test. Now she can enjoy her weekend. She knows she will graduate.

071

Summary
The information in a good dictionary is important to people who want to use language well.

Topic
A Dictionary

Main idea
A dictionary will give you lots of information.

072

Mark couldn't find his car keys this morning. He looked everywhere in his apartment for them. Then he realized that he'd left them in the car and locked the doors. He tried to open one of the doors with a coat hanger, but it didn't work. He didn't have time to get a new key, so he rode his bicycle to the office.

073

Summary
You can save money by eating and by planning your meals before you go to the grocery store.

Topic
Two Tips for Shopping at the Grocery Store

Main idea
Eat and plan your meals before you go to the grocery store, and you can save money.

074

1. How many students are there in the classroom?
2. How many notebooks does she buy in a year?
3. How many words do you learn every day?
4. How many seconds are there in a minute?
5. How many meals does she have in a day?

075

1. Larry wants to study Korean.
2. Greg doesn't want to swim.
3. Rosa doesn't want to drink coffee.
4. Ann wants to buy a novel.

5. Scott and Liz want to go abroad for study.

076

Summary
Andy spends a lot of time working in his yard. It really keeps him busy.

Topic
Doing Something in a Yard

Main idea
Andy has done and will do something in his yard.

077

Summary
Mary didn't take her umbrella to work. It started to rain while she was walking home, and she got very wet.

Topic
Mary's Walking in a Changeable Weather

Main idea
Mary didn't take a umbrella to work with her, so she got very wet while walking home.

078

Yesterday a teacher phoned from my son's school. He said, "Your son hurt his leg. Can you come to the school right now?" "I'll be there in a few minutes," I said. I left the house, ran to my car, and drove to the school. I got there in fifteen minutes.

079

5-2-3-1-4

Angela needed to buy a few things.
She counted her money.
She didn't have much.
Then she walked to the bank.
She cashed a check there and got some money.
From the bank, she took a bus downtown.

080

1-2-3-4-5

Lorena and Kim work in a hotel.
They clean the rooms every day.
First, they wash the bathrooms.
Then they change the sheets, blankets and pillows.
Their work is not so hard, so they like it.

081

Howard and Helen went to a new restaurant. The food was tasty. The service was good. They were both satisfied and decided to come again.

082

Summary
Carl was tired after a long hard day at work. The phone rang as he was leaving, but he was too tired to answer it.

Topic
A Long Hard Day for Carl

Main idea
Carl had a long hard and tiring day.

083

1. Who was in Canada two weeks ago?
2. What was on the table yesterday?
3. Where was Cathy last night?
4. When were you in England?
5. Who wasn't in class yesterday?

084

Tim hurt his right knee last week. He saw the doctor and he took his medicine. Tim didn't come to class for two days. He went to the doctor's office again. The doctor looked at his knee and put medicine on it. The next day his knee was all right.

085

1-4-3-2-5

The work day in Seoul starts between 7:00 and 9:00.
Most people get up between 5:30 and 6:00.
They get dressed and eat breakfast then they start for work.
Most of the people drive their cars to work, but some take the bus or subway.

There are some people who live so far, they have to take a train.

86

Ben had to mail a package. He had the address, but he didn't have a stamp. He had to go to the post office for it. When he got there, he had to stand in line.

87

Can anyone tell you what causes sleep? We know that all people and all animals need sleep. Some people think that plants also need sleep. Not many people can say what causes sleep, but all of us need it.

88

Lunch at American restaurants is usually served in three parts. The first part is a salad with coffee or tea. The next part is the meat and two vegetables all on one plate. Hot rolls or some kind of bread is usually served with the meal. Dessert is served last, and you usually have to pay extra for it.

89

Summary
George missed his dinner yesterday. He was playing baseball and didn't want to come inside when it was ready.

Topic
George's playing baseball and missing dinner

Main idea
George played baseball with his friends and he missed his dinner.

90

1. Joe ate 2 cans of tomato for breakfast.
2. Nick bought 1 tube of toothpaste at the store.
3. There is 1 quart of milk in the container.
4. There are 8 ounces of juice in the bottle.
5. They needed 4 gallons of juice.

91

Summary
In the late 1800's, people in U.S. and Switzerland made machines that made many kinds of clocks. These machines made the clocks faster and cheaper than men could.

Topic
A Variety of Clocks

Main idea
Many kinds of clocks made in U.S. and Switzerland in the late 1800's were more convenient than man-made ones.

92

Mike loves to cook. He cooks all kinds of dishes, but his favorite dishes are desserts. He says cooking is very relaxing. When he is working in the kitchen, he thinks only about cooking. He doesn't think about work or bad thing. He can bake big and beautiful cakes with fruit or with chocolate.

93

The Lucky Department <u>had</u> a big sale <u>yesterday</u>. They <u>had</u> a lot of good deals. In the variety store, they <u>had</u> plastic dishes and glass items for much less than usual. Silk skirts <u>were</u> 20% off, and cotton clothes <u>were</u> 45% off. The discount on the jewelry <u>was</u> the best. Gold rings, gold chains, silver bracelets, and copper earrings <u>sold</u> for 50% off.

94

3-5-1-4-2

Karen wanted to rent a new apartment.

First, the manager showed her a one-bedroom apartment.

She didn't want it because it was too small.

Then she looked at a two-bedroom apartment.

She put a deposit on it.

95

1-5-2-3-4

Mark and Sara took a vacation.

They took a long trip and stayed overnight in many nice hotels.

They went sightseeing every day and took a lot

pictures of mountains and lakes.
They used many rolls of film.
Mark and Sara both enjoyed their trip.

096
The tough man bought a new book from the old clerk in the bookstore. He took it home and read it slowly. He thought it was a very boring book.

097
Because Chris is an automobile mechanic, he can fix a car's air conditioner, replace the battery, fix or replace the radiator, or repair any problems with a car. Because he used to assemble cars for a car company, he can now figure out any problems with a car.

098
Aluminum is a powerful electrical conductor. It is used in the production of electrical circuits and wires. Aluminum is not as good as silver for conducting electricity, but it is a lot cheaper. Besides silver is too beautiful to use for ugly wires that are covered by insulation. Silver is good for making jewelry; aluminum is better for electrical production.

099
Summary
Paula's in class, but she's not reading her textbook. She's thinking about her vacation in Florida.

Topic
Paula's Florida Trip

Main idea
Paula enjoyed her vacation to Florida and is now thinking about her trip.

100
Max owns a gas station. He works very hard. He has to repair cars. His brother helps him. The work is difficult. He makes a lot of money. He and his family are happy because the gas station is theirs.

101
Computers can do many things these days. First of all, they can add numbers. They can also print things fast and well. You can send letters to people all over the world. You can find information for school or business. You can also shop for things on the computer, and you can watch a movie on the computer.

102
Script
A skunk sleeps during the day and looks for food at night. It eats small animals, birds, eggs, fruit, and other things. But its favorite meal is bugs. A skunk can't see very well, but it has very good ears and a good nose that help it find food and stay safe.

Title
A Skunk

Rewrite
A skunk sleeps in the day and looks for food at night. It eats animals, birds, eggs, and fruit. It's favorite meal is bugs. It can't see well, but it has good ears and a good nose that helps it find food and stay safe.

103
Summary
Sally doesn't get much exercises at her job, so she tries to run in the country every day after work. She enjoys running there. She's always relaxed after she runs.

Topic
Sally's Staying Healthy

Main idea
Sally stays healthy running after work.

104
The new car was noisy. It really made awful noises. Ted bought it on credit for his son. He thinks a tune-up will help it.

105
Summary
Jack took his car to ACE GARAGE. Mike, the

mechanic, worked on the car for five hours. He fixed a lot of things and Jack will be satisfied.

Topic
Repairing a Car

Main idea
Mike, the mechanic, repaired a car by four steps.

106

David likes to play baseball. He doesn't like to play basketball. He plays baseball with his friends on Saturday mornings. David likes to watch baseball games, too. Last Sunday there was a big baseball game on television. Did David watch it? He did.

107

3-4-1-5-2

Tony's first stop was the drugstore.

He picked up his mother's medicine there.

From the drugstore, he went to the grocery store.

There he got some chicken for his family's dinner.

His last stop was the post office.

108

Summary
Ken's family all live together in a large old house. They help each other and work together happily.

Topic
a large happy family

Main idea
Ken and her husband have a large and happy family. All of the members of their family are working together.

109

3-6-1-5-2-4

A: The weather's terrible. If you're leaving, you should leave soon.

B: I expect to leave at noon if it clears up.

A: If this rain freezes, it'll be dangerous to drive.

B: Yes, but the police will close the roads if it gets too bad.

A: What'll you do if that happens?

B: Well, if they do that, I'll stop until it clears up.

110

Mr. Brown and his grandson <u>have</u> a very special friendship. Tim <u>is</u> very special to Mr. Brown because he <u>is</u> such a smart boy. He always <u>has</u> a smile on his face and a pleasant word for everyone. The boy and the old man <u>spend</u> many hours together fishing in the lake near their home. When Tim <u>gets</u> sick, Mr. Brown <u>is</u> worried.

111

Summary
Karen likes her job because she meets interesting people from different places around the world. She hopes to visit their countries one day.

Topic
A Cashier in a Hotel Restaurant

Main idea
Karan is a cashier in a hotel restaurant and she likes her job very much.

112

Mary does the same thing when she comes home in the evenings. She picks up the mail before she goes into the house. She doesn't open it until she changes her clothes. She reads the mail before she turns on the TV. When she finishes with the mail, she cooks her dinner. Then she eats her dinner while she watches TV.

113

Script
I remember when I made a bet on a basketball game. I made the bet with my friend, Tony. I bet him ten dollars that my son's high school basketball team would beat his son's high school team. Well, I won the bet. My son's team won by two points. I was very happy and also very proud. You see, my son scored the goal that won the game.

Title
Betting

Rewrite
One day I made a bet on a basketball game. I bet my friend, Tony, ten dollars that my son's high school basketball team would beat his son's team. I won ten dollars from my friend because my son's team won. I was very happy and proud because my son' goal won the game.

114

Summary
Keeping up with world and local news is important to Alex. He thinks this makes him a good businessman.

Topic
News from Newspapers

Main idea
Alex keeps up with world and local news from newspapers.

115

1. Can you buy me some stamps?
2. Did Mary send Pam a postcard?
3. Does the florist send you some flowers?
4. Will Mary send me the check?
5. Would you bring me a cup of tea?

116

Ann went to a clothing store last week. She bought a blue coat for the winter. She wants to wear the coat to the October dance. She has a blue dress and blue shoes. Ann went to the store again this morning. She bought gloves. What color are her gloves? Are they blue, too?

117

Mr. Smith <u>got</u> up at 8 o'clock on Saturday. He <u>slept</u> later because he <u>didn't</u> have to go to work. After he <u>got</u> dressed, he <u>ate</u> breakfast. He <u>had</u> two eggs, toast, and coffee. After breakfast, he <u>went</u> to the gym. Then, he <u>went</u> home and <u>watched</u> TV. About 19:30, he <u>cooked</u> his dinner. Then, he <u>called</u> his friend, Andy, and <u>made</u> plans for the evening

118

4-1-2-5-3

Last night our family had an early dinner.

After dinner, we went to a movie.

After the movie, we stopped at the snack bar.

We ordered some ice cream there.

We ate our ice cream in the bar.

119

1-2-4-5-6-3

Mark's car started to pull to the right.

He got out of the car and looked at his tire.

It was flat!

He jacked up the car and loosened the lugs.

The car started moving and he fell off the jack.

Next time, he'll call the garage.

120

Summary
The first mechanical washing machine was made by Hamilton Smith in 1858. In 1910, the first electric washing machine was made by Alva J. Fisher. These machines are fantastic because they wash clothes faster than people can.

Topic
Washing Machines

Main idea
Washing machines are very convenient to wash clothes.

121

5-2-1-8-4-6-7-3

Roger wanted to take a vacation.

First, he went to a travel agency.

They had information about many places.

He decided to go to Rome.

The agency made the reservation in Rome for him.

Then they sent him to the airport for his tickets.

After he picked them up, he went home back.

Thanks to the agency, he could start his

vacation in two days.

122

The tall girl bought a new pencil from the old clerk at the fancy store. She took it home and slowly sharpened it. She thought it was a pretty pencil and she liked it very much.

123

Summary
Newspapers are important, and millions of people read them every day. People can get their papers three ways. They can get them from a newsstand or a store or a vending machine, or have them brought to their homes.

Topic
How We Get Our Newspapers

Main
There are several ways to get newspapers.

124

My girlfriend, Sarah likes to listen to and play classical music. She plays the violin in an orchestra. I don't like to listen to or play classical music. I would rather listen to rock music, so I never go to my girlfriend's concerts.

125

Swimming, bicycling and running are three very popular sports. Some people like to do all three sports in one race. They can do all three in a triathlon race. Triathlon means "three sports." In a triathlon the people must first swim for a mile(1.6km). Then they must ride a bicycle for about 10 miles(16km). And then they must run for three miles(4.8km). You must be a very strong person to win a triathlon!

126

Script
People made candles a long time ago. Thousands of years ago, people learned that pieces of wood burned longer if they covered them with animal grease. The Egyptians used cloth and animal grease in small bowls as candles. The Romans were the first people to make candles that look like the candles we use today. The Romans made them from grease.

Title
The Candles

Rewrite
People made first candles a long time ago. Thousands of years ago, somebody put grease on pieces of wood to make them burn longer. Egyptians used cloth and grease in bowls as candles. The Romans were the first people who made candles like the candles today. They made candles from grease.

127

Summary
There are things you should do when on vacation. Check your car, have the right tools with you, and drive carefully. If you do, you'll have a good and safe trip.

Topic
Doing Things Before Vacation

Main idea
If you do several things you should be before you go on vacation, you'll have a good and safe trip.

128

Summary
A Korean went to the bank today to learn what to do with his money. He learned about savings and checking accounts. He also learned how to fill out deposit slips. He feels good and satisfied.

Topic
A Bank

Main idea
Aliens must know several things to deal with money in a bank in the United States.

129

Summary
Charlie had a problem with his car the day before yesterday. He took it to a repair shop to be fixed. The car had overheated. Today he is checking to see if it is ready.

Topic

Charlie Left His Car Repaired

Main idea

Charlie had a problem with his car and took it to a repair shop.

130

1. Harry went to the bank after lunch. He bought a money order and traveler's checks. He wanted to cash a check. The clerk asked for his ID card. But he didn't have it. It was at home.
2. I went to the drug store this morning. I bought some medicines and a comb. I had to cash a check. The clerk asked for my identification. But I didn't have it. It was at the hotel.
3. Julie went to the grocery store yesterday. She bought some fruits and milk. She wanted to cash a check. The clerk asked for her driver's license. But she didn't have it. It was at home.
4. Tom and Al went to the drug store Monday night. They bought some medicines and film. They had to cash a check. They clerk asked for Tom's ID card. But he didn't have it. It was at the hotel.
5. Harry went to the department store yesterday. He bought a shirt and a toothpaste. He wanted to cash a check. The clerk asked for Harry's identification. But he didn't have it. It was in the car.

131

Paul likes to take trips. He takes two trips every year. The first trip is to Wyoming. He visits his father and mother. His second trip is to a new city. He likes to see a new city every year. He went to Chicago last year. He wants to go to New York this year.

132

2-4-3-1

A: Hi, Sony. What have you decided to do about the job offers?

B: I've decided to take the one in San Francisco.

A: Instead of the one in L.A.? Why did you do that?

B: Because the pay is better, and I can take some courses at the university there.

A: You'll enjoy the university. When do you plan to leave?

B: The end of the month.

A: Where are you going to live in San Francisco?

B: I haven't made up my mind yet. I'll have to look at apartments.

133

Helen was on vacation. She bought a local newspaper. She wanted to find a good restaurant. She was hungry, and she wanted to eat before she went back to her hotel.

134

Script

People have been having birthday parties for hundreds of years. One of the first birthday parties happened in Egypt about three thousand years ago. The pharaoh, the head of the country, had a party for all the people on his birthday. After this, people began to have parties, but they were for important men only. Today, Parties for men, women, and children are popular in many countries.

Title

Birthday Parties Have Been Popular

Rewrite

People have had birthday parties for many years. The first party was in Egypt 3,000 years ago. The pharaoh, head of the country, had a party for his people on his birthday. After this, people had parties, but only important men had them. Today parties are popular in many countries.

135

Summary

Different kinds of people get together for different reasons. Get-togethers can be for fun, business, parties for happy things.

Topic

Getting Together

Main idea
People get together for different reasons.

136

Summary
There are a lot of commercials on American TV, but most people don't like them. Commercials make a lot of money for businesses, so commercials are here to stay.

Topic
Commercials

Main idea
There are lots of commercials on American TV to get you to buy something.

137

1. Susan went to Korea last week. She traveled by plane. Her friends met her at the airport. They took her to the hotel.
2. Becky went to Houston last week. She traveled by bus. Her family met her at the station. They took her to their house.
3. The athletes went to Chicago yesterday. They traveled by plane. Their fans met them at the airport. They took them to the restaurant.
4. My Boss went to China last year. He traveled by plane. His men met him at the airport. They took him to the company.
5. Tony went to New York last week. He traveled by car. His friends met him at the Bank of America. They took him to the hotel.

138

Betty and Henry went to a dance last Saturday. Betty wore a long pink dress. Henry wore a black suit. They danced all night long. They were very happy. They were very sore the next day. Their feet hurt. Their arms hurt. Their heads hurt. They slept all morning long. They were all right on Monday.

139

5-2-3-4-1

I haven't decided when to take my vacation yet. I can go in the summer, or I can go in the winter. If I go in the summer, I can enjoy the sun at the beach.
But I will enjoy the snow if I go in the winter.
When do you think I should go?

140

Script
Jane and her younger brother Tom volunteered to help at the hospital last week. At first they were both nervous, but after a few minutes they became more relaxed. They were able to visit the patients in their rooms, talk to them, and take them their lunches. Jane and Tom enjoyed volunteering their time. In fact, they want to do it again next week.

Title
Volunteering

Rewrite
Jane and her brother Tom spent some time with patients at a hospital last week. They volunteered their time. They visited the patients and talked to them and took their lunches to them. They had a good time and want to go again next week.

141

Summary
Garages usually guarantee their work because they don't want to lose customers. Most unhappy customers won't return.

Topic
Garages for Customers

Main idea
Because garages must satisfy their customers, they have to try their best.

142

Script
Mr. Bush didn't feel well when he woke up Friday morning. He had a bad pain in his back. By 10 o'clock he called the doctor because the pain had gotten worse. The doctor examined him and told him that he should have an operation immediately. By 2 o'clock that afternoon, the doctor was operating on Mr. Bush.

Title
Bush's Backache

Rewrite
Friday morning, Mr. Bush had a pain in his back. It became worse a few hours later. He called the doctor. The doctor said that he should have an operation right away. The doctor operated on him that afternoon.

143

Summary
Drivers should stop regularly on long trips. Those who don't take breaks can become tired and cause accidents.

Topic
A Break Necessary to a Long-trip Driver

Main idea
A long-trip driver needs to take a break, or he may cause a terrible accident.

144

1. Paula has a new car. She keeps it in the garage. She uses it to drive to school.
2. Sony has a new car. He keeps it in the garage. He uses it to drive to work.
3. My parents have a new couch. They keep it in the living room. They use it to sit on.
4. Mark has a new radio. He keeps it in the bedroom. He uses it to listen to music.
5. Ben and I have a new refrigerator. We keep it in the kitchen. We use it to keep food cold.

145

Saturday morning Harry made a long distance phone call to his family. His mother answered the phone. Harry said, "Hi, mom. How are you?" She said, "Harry! It's Harry on the phone!" Then Harry's father, his brother, and his brother's wife picked up the phone. They talked for about ten minutes.

146

Mr. and Mrs. Clinton <u>will take</u> their vacation <u>next</u> month. They <u>will drive</u> to Canada with some friends. The drive to Canada <u>will take</u> four days. They <u>will stay</u> in some very nice motels on the way. They <u>will eat</u> at some wonderful restaurants; they <u>will dance</u> to some nice music; and they <u>will see</u> some beautiful things.

147

2-4-1-5-3

Jerry wrote a letter to his friend yesterday.

After he signed the letter, he put it in the envelope.

Then he wrote his friend's address on the back of the envelope and his return address on the front.

Then he put a stamp on the envelope and left with the letter in his hand.

He went to the post office and mailed the letter.

148

4-2-3-1-5

I woke up this morning and decided to go shopping.

I needed some drapes for the bedroom.

I went to WHITES department store.

They had some pretty ones.

I bought them, took them home and hung them up.

149

John's roommate is a healthy man. He works out at the men's gym every day. Usually, he takes his gym clothes with him. But yesterday, he forgot, and he had to borrow someone's clothes.

150

Captain Jackson does what is right because he's honorable. He treats officers with respect and always salutes them. He obeys his seniors and follows all the rules. His orders are reasonable and he treats his subordinates with respect. Maybe Captain Jackson will be a police chief someday.

151

Script
Paul was talking about his aunt the other day. He remembered that she used to spend the

entire day in her kitchen. She would make bread, pies, and cakes and would prepare the most delicious dinners that he had ever eaten. She would also write her own recipes and give them to her friends. Paul seemed very happy when he was talking about his aunt. She must have been a wonderful person.

Title
Paul's Aunt Was a Wonderful Cook

Rewrite
Paul talked about his aunt the other day. She used to make bread, pies, and cakes. She would also make delicious dinners. She used to write recipes and give them to her friends. Paul loved his aunt very much. She was a wonderful person.

152

Summary
Man has been interested in the ocean for a long time, but we don't know much about the ocean. Today we have new tools to study the ocean, and it may offer the world many things for the future.

Topic
The Ocean

Main idea
The ocean has been frightening and dangerous and will be of service to man.

153

Summary
The flu lasts a few days or longer and causes a variety of symptoms. Medicine, fruit juice, and rest can help when you have it.

Topic
The Symptoms of the Flu

Main idea
The flu last a few days or longer and result in various symptoms. Medicine, fruit juice, and rest can be of help when you get it.

154

Script
People at North Dakota University studied the decisions that men and women make. They found out that men change their minds two to three times more often than women. Most women take a longer time to make a decision, but when they finally make it, they stay with it.

Answer
1. People at North Dakota University studied the decisions of men and women.
2. Men change their mind more often than women.
3. Women take longer to make a decision.
4. Women stay with their decisions longer than men.

Rewrite
People at North Dakota University studied the decisions of men and women. They found out that men change their minds more often than women, but women take longer to make a decision. Women stay with their decisions longer than men.

155

Summary
Sizes of clothes are different in each country because each country uses the average measurements of its own people. So when you are in another country, it's best to try on clothes before you buy them.

Topic
Different Countries Use Different Measurements for Clothes

Main idea
Measurements are different in each country, so it's best to try on clothes before you buy them.

156

Summary
There are glass stones that look like diamonds which people use in jewelry when they can't afford real diamonds. Professional jewelers can tell the difference between the stones and diamonds with a quick look, but other people can't.

Topic
Glass Stones

Main idea
Glass stones look like real diamonds, but there is a different between them.

157
4-2-3-1-5
I went to the library the other day.
First I selected books about the atmosphere.
Next I looked at the books I had selected.
After that, I picked put the best and checked them out.
With my arms filled with books, I finally went back to my room to start my research.

158
3-2-5-1-4
Mr. Brown was driving home from work one dark, rainy night.
He thought he was the only person on the highway, but when he came to the top of a hill, he saw that there was an accident on the road ahead.
He drove to the nearest house and used the telephone there to call the police.
He tried to return to the accident because he was worried about the people who might be hurt, but he couldn't find it again; the cars weren't there anymore.
Then Mr. Brown really began to worry.

159
Paul needed some money. He went to the bank, but it was closed. He asked a man for some advice. The man said, "Use the machine for withdrawals or deposits."

160
Script
Some people spend a lot of time and a lot of money trying to lose weight. They may go to expensive health clubs. They may try and unusual diet. At a health club, they follow a careful diet and do daily exercises. Each person may have his or her own special diet and exercise plan.

Answers
1. People spend a lot of time and money when try to lose weight.
2. They go to expensive health clubs.
3. They try unusual diet.
4. They follow a careful diet and do daily exercises.
5. Everyone may have a special diet and exercise plan.

Rewrite
People spend a lot of time and money when they try to lose weight. They go to expensive health clubs. They try unusual diets. At a health clubs, they follow a careful diet and do daily exercises. Everyone may have a special diet and exercise plan.

161
Summary
There's a new item to help prevent accidents. It tells a driver the temperature of the road ahead and if there might be ice or snow on the road.

Topic
A New Item to Tell a Drive the Road Condition in Winter

Main idea
A new item helps to prevent a driver from road accidents in winter.

162
Summary
Metal plates on the ceilings of buildings spray water and chemicals to put out fires. The alarms will call the fire department.

Topic
Sprays - Small Metal Plates on the Ceiling

Main idea
Sprays can help to save our lives when there is a fire in a room or building.

163
1. My wife drove to Miami Beach last weekend. She took pictures of trees and lakes. She went to many attractions. The weather was very sunny and the food was very delicious.

She stayed three days and didn't want to come back.

2. Harry flew to Russia last week. He took pictures of snow. He went to many diners. The days were very cold and the food was sometimes awful. He stayed one week and wanted to return.

3. Mr. and Mrs. White traveled by ship to England last year. They took pictures of many different things. They went to many stores. The nights were sometimes rainy and the food was never good. They stayed one week and wanted to come back.

4. Ken and I traveled by bus to California last summer. We took pictures of trees and lakes. We went to many stores. The sky was always clear and the food was very good. We stayed six weeks and didn't want to come back.

5. Four doctors flew to New York last month. They took pictures of tall buildings. They went to many stores. The weather was sometimes cold and the food was often bad. They stayed one week and wanted to return.

164

Steve walked into his office yesterday. He looked at his desk. His pens, pencils, and calendar were there, but his phone wasn't on his desk. "Where's my phone?" Then someone said, "You forgot to pay for your phone this month, Steve. They came and picked it up."

165

5-4-6-2-3-1

First he bought materials; then he measured and cut the wood.

He nailed the shelves in before he put the back on the bookcases.

Last of all, he sanded the bookcases.

166

6-2-4-7-5-3-1

Jack is getting ready for a final term exam tomorrow.

First, he'll study with Max for about three hours.

Then he'll have lunch and relax for about an hour and a half.

After lunch he'll study again until 5 o'clock.

After dinner he'll rest and listen to the music.

Then he'll go to bed by 10 o'clock.

He thinks this is a wonderful study schedule.

167

Script

You can increase your chances for living longer. First, by not smoking, you can add one and a half years. Second, by exercising every day, you can add one year. If you use your seat belt each time you drive, you can add six months. Finally, if you lose extra weight that you have, you can add three and a half months.

Answer

1. The topic is how you can increase your chances for living longer.
2. The first thing you can do is not to smoke.
3. The second way to increase your chances of living longer is to exercise every day.
4. Use seat belt each time you drive and add six months.
5. Finally, you should lose any extra weight to live longer.

Rewrite

You can increase your chances for living longer. The first thing you can do is not to smoke. The second way to increase your chances of living longer is to exercise every day. Use seat belts each time you drive and add six months. Finally, you should lose any extra weight to live longer.

168

Summary

Mr. Goosen needs to get a Florida driver's license. He has learned that people must wear a seat belt, that children under four must be in a safety seat, and that people must have insurance.

Topic

A Florida Driver's License

Main idea

Mr. Goosen studies the traffic laws to get a Florida driver's license.

169

Summary

Dentists used gold to repair and fill teeth for many years because it was easy to work with, and it lasted a long time. But today they are using man-made materials instead of gold because they are cheaper.

Topic

Gold for Repairing and Filling Teeth

Main idea

Gold was need for teeth a lot yesterday, but today man-made materials are more used than gold.

170

Summary

Man needs machines to study the ocean. There were machines in the past, but today we have a better machine. It's a vehicle with large windows that can move and stay underwater a long time.

Topic

A Machine to Study the Ocean

Main idea

Today we have a better machine for studying the ocean than past.

171

1. Mary went to the grocery store. She bought cookies for her dessert. They cost a lot. She also went to the bookstore and bought some books.
2. Paula went to the market. She bought fish for her cat. It didn't cost much. She also went to the post office and mailed some letters.
3. My father and I went to the drugstore. We bought toothpastes for our teeth. They didn't cost a lot. We also went to the library and got many books.
4. Mr. and Mrs. Bush went to the market. They bought food for their lunch. It cost much. They also went to the bank and cashed a check.
5. Kevin went to the drugstore. He bought films for his trip. They cost much. He also went to the bank and cashed a check.

172

1-2-3-4-5-6

Sally and Diane like to travel.

Usually they travel by plane.

When they arrive at the airport, they rent a car.

They do this because it is cheaper to go sightseeing by car than by taxi.

When they go sightseeing, they learn a lot about the people and places.

This new information about the people and places is exciting for Sally and Diane.

173

People like to shop at a mall. They can park in the parking lot. There are clothing stores and many other kinds of stores. There are many places to eat at while you shop. It's nice to go shopping at a mall.

174

Summary

Education is important, but you can learn more at a job than you can in school. In college, students should try to work in their fields. The experience will help them decide if they like it and help them find jobs later.

Topic

The Importance of Education in a Job

Main idea

When we work at a job, we learn more than we do in school. So while in college, we should try to work hard in our field.

175

Summary

Polyester is a man-made material, and we use it in many things from automobile tires to the clothes we wear. For example, Polyester is very strong enough to last a long time and it is used to make clothes we wear.

Topic

Polyester

Main idea

People use polyester to make many things-from

automobile tires to the clothes they wear.

176

Summary
Samuel Colt was interested in guns. He got new ideas for a gun on a ship and in India. He finally made his new gun because he looked for new ideas and never stopped trying.

Topic
Samuel Colt's New Ideas for Guns

Main idea
Samuel Colt looked for new ideas for guns without stopping and finally made a weapon that could repeat shots without reloading.

177

Do you borrow anything from others? Do you lend anything to others? Of course, you do. So do most of us. So do western people, but in the west, there are more principles than in the east. You can borrow things from others, but you must return them later no matter whether it's one dollar or only a pencil. Moreover, you must make sure that the thing is as good as before. If you break it, you must pay for it! Do you think they are reasonable?

178

3-7-1-4-6-2-8-5

Thursday morning Ted had a headache when he got up.

By 9 o'clock he had a cough, a runny nose, and a temperature.

At 10:00 he called the doctor's office.

The woman on the phone asked Ted about his symptoms.

She also asked about the date of his last checkup.

Ted answered that he had a physical 3 weeks ago.

She gave him a 2 o'clock appointment.

Ted sneezed, coughed, and said ,"Thanks. See you at 2 o'clock."

179

Mike's appearance is very important in his job. He is a businessman in whom people place their trust. He must look neat, responsible, and dependable while he is at work. Because his job is so demanding, on weekends he relaxes. He lets his beard grow and wears old clothes. He doesn't look like the same man everyone trusts and depends on at work.

180

Script
The year 1976 was an important year for people in the United States. First, it was the 200th birthday of the country. Second, in 1976, women began to go to the four U.S. military academies. There was a total of 355 women who went that first year. 1976 is a year most American women, as well as men, won't forget.

Answer
1. The year 1976 was an important year for people in the United States.
2. It was 200th birthday of the country.
3. Also, women entered the U.S. military academies that year.
4. 355 women attended the academies that year.
5. The year 1976 was a year American women and men won't forget.

Rewrite
The year 1976 was an important year for people in the United States. It was the 200th birthday of the country. Also, in that year, women entered the U.S. military academies. 355 women attended the academies that year. The year 1976 was a year American women and men won't forget.

181

Summary
People began using vending machines in the U.S. in the 1890s. These machines sold gum, stamps and peanuts. Vending machines today sell unusual things, and some can talk.

Topic
A Vending Machine

Main idea

We can buy usual and unusual things from vending machines.

182

Summary
Your home is a dangerous place. Careless people cause many accidents in their homes. People need to be careful and practice being safe in their homes.

Topic
One of the Most Dangerous Places, Home

Main idea
A home can be a dangerous place, so we need to be careful in our homes.

183

Summary
Some English words come from other languages. The word "gun" comes from Norwegian. The word "rifle" comes from German.

Topic
Some English Borrowed Words

Main idea
Some English words come from other languages.

184

1. Mr. and Mrs. Brown wanted to eat lunch at a good restaurant last night. They sat at a table for a few minutes. The waitress was very nice, and the food cost only a little money. They stayed there and ate a good meal.

2. Alicia wanted to eat a snack at small snack bar this morning. She stood in line for a long time. The waiter was very slow, and the food cost a lot of money. She went home.

3. My uncle wanted to eat dinner at a new cafeteria last night. He sat at a table for twenties minutes. The waiter was very slow, but the food cost only a little. He stayed there and ate a good meal.

4. I wanted to eat dinner at a small diner yesterday. I stood in line for a long time. The waitress was very young and the food cost only a little money. I stayed there and ate a good meal.

5. My nephew wanted to eat breakfast at a crowded cafeteria this morning. He stood in line for a long time. The waiter was very fast, and the food cost only a little money. He stayed there and ate a good meal.

185

Thanksgiving Day is a holiday in the USA. It is on the fourth Thursday of November. On that day, families and friends get together for a turkey dinner. People leave work early on Wednesday afternoon and drive their cars to distant places for a family reunion. There was a story about Thanksgiving Day. When the first English settlers arrived in America in 1621, they didn't have enough food. With the Indians' help, they had a good harvest. The English invited the Indians to their dinner in order to give thanks to them for their help and to God.

186

When Sony <u>visited</u> his uncle in St. Louis, he <u>did</u> the same things every day. First, he <u>ate</u> a big breakfast. Then, he <u>helped</u> his uncle clean up the house. After that, they <u>took</u> a trip to the gym for a two-hour workout. In the afternoon they <u>took</u> a one-hour nap, and then they <u>played</u> cards until it <u>was</u> time for dinner. After dinner, they <u>took</u> a three-mile walk. When they <u>got</u> home, it <u>was</u> time for a shower and bed. Sony <u>was</u> in real good shape when he <u>got</u> home from his uncle's house.

187

2-3-4-1-5-6

Judy helped Tom build new bookcases.
First Judy helped him measure the wood.
Then she held the wood while Tom sawed it.
After they had lunch, Judy took the kids to the swimming pool.

188

1-5-2-6-4-3-7

Mark is having a dinner party this evening.
First, he'll serve a cream soup with cheese.
Second, he'll serve a salad of tomatoes and

onions.

Then for the meat dish, he'll serve chicken and vegetables.

He always uses carrots when he makes his dish.

Finally, for dessert he'll serve fruit and ice cream.

That kind of meal is a lot of work, but Mark likes dinner parties.

189

A little boy carelessly walked across a busy street. At the same time, a big car was traveling in the boy's direction. Because he was tired, the child didn't see the car. But the man in the car was a good driver, and he saw the child right away. He stopped the car, got out, and picked up the tired child. Then he took him home.

190

Mr. White fell asleep at 10 a.m. while he was on duty because he had very little slept the night before. He had taken some pills for losing weight which had made him nervous and had kept him awake. The friend who had recommended the pills didn't tell him that the pills might cause problems. Mr. White learned not to take medication without checking it out with a doctor.

191

Summary
The Astrodome in Houston, Texas was the first stadium with a cover. It has room for 66,000 people and has a floor of man-made grass. It's the "astrodome" because it's in the city that is the home of the astronauts.

Topic
The Astrodome in Houston, Texas

Main idea
The Astrodome in Houston, Texas is the first dome-stadium with man-made grass.

192

Summary
There are many kinds of grasses. Man and animals eat some of the grasses. Grass is also important to keep the land from becoming a desert.

Topic
The Importance of Grasses

Main idea
Grasses are very important to man and animals, for they give food to them. Next grasses keep the land from becoming a desert.

193

Summary
Traffic signals work by three different ways. One kind works with clocks. Another kind works with wires under the streets. A third kind works with buttons that people push.

Topic
Three Kinds of the Traffic Signals

Main idea
Traffic signals work by three different ways.

194

Summary
Andy had been studying for two hours. He was very tired. He got up from his desk and looked out the window. He saw some people who reminded him of his family. A few minutes later, he began to study again.

Topic
Andy's Studying

Main idea
Andy studied and often took a rest, thinking of his own family.

195

I see something that is made of plastic. It's dark brown and white. I look at it when I want to know when the break will be. What is it? It's the clock.

196

Frank felt very warm during the last period of class. His head hurt, and his stomach was upset. He couldn't keep his mind on the lesson. He was also worried about a dinner invitation for that evening.

197

Tina saw items that people used for hunting and fishing hundreds of years ago. She also saw the type of clothes that people wore. She saw the dishes that people used for cooking and eating. The history of the people was interesting.

198

Mary has a broom, a mop, a scrub brush, and a cloth for cleaning windows. There are many apartments in the building. It will be hard work, but maybe she can buy some food this week.

199

Jenifer sliced the large, red strawberries into a bowl. She added some sugar and thick cream. She put the strawberries and cream on a slice of chocolate cake. The dessert was ready just in time - the doorbell rang.

200

Tina was playing tennis when she twisted her knee and fell. The coach took her out of the game immediately. Tina was angry because she didn't want to stop playing.

201

Frank and patty are standing on a corner in downtown New York. Frank has a camera around his neck, and Patty is looking at a map. Both of them are wearing shorts.

202

Mark and Ellen went to a concert. Their seats were located about the middle of the theater. They could hear the orchestra very well. They could see all parts of the stage. They were glad to get those seats.

203

Alice saw a musical for the first time last week. The story was good, but she didn't like the actor and actress singing every few minutes. She didn't like the actors dancing. She thought the music was unnecessary.

204

Jane started English class four weeks ago. At the end of the first week, her listening was poor and her speaking was also poor. She studied a lot of words the second week, and could understand what the teacher was saying a little better. At the end of the second week, her listening was good, but her speaking was still poor. By the end of the third week, her listening was good, and her speaking was also good. Now, at the end of fourth week, Jane's listening is very good, but her speaking is still only good. She knows she still needs to practice speaking.

205

Monday morning, Alex had only $50.00 in his wallet for the whole week. That day he bought lunch and a newspaper for $5.00. The next day, he met a friend who owed him $10.00. Alex was glad to get the money back. On Wednesday, he returnd the jacket to the clothing store and received a refund for $45.00. The next evening, Alex took Betty to dinner, and spent $20.00 that evening. On Saturday, he paid $10.00 for his laundry bill.

206

On Sunday, October 4, Mr. Howard will have dinner with his wife. The day after tomorrow, he must return books to the library and buy a new car. The next day, he will meet Jane for lunch. October 9, Mr. Howard has to go to a wedding at 6 p.m. The next week on Tuesday, he will go to the clinic for his annual checkup. The next day on Wednesday, he'll take a test for driver's license. Finally, on October 15, Mr. Howard can begin his two weeks of vacation.

207

Scott filled out the application for a visa. He put his documents in order and looked at his watch. He was ready to leave as soon as he received his visa from the woman behind the desk.

208

Mark and Paula are getting married on Friday.

They'll invite their relatives and friends to the wedding. They'll have a barbecue supper for all the guests. There will also be a large wedding cake and a lot to drink. After the meal, everyone will stay for the dance.

209

Mr. and Mrs. Brown could see the snow on the mountain tops. They could see the rivers like thin, narrow stripes below. The green valleys that looked so large and wide from the ground now looked small and narrow. The clouds were so close they could almost touch them.

210

Some students were sitting outside on the ground and eating hamburgers and potato salad. At the picnic table, other students were helping themselves to soda pop and putting French fries and catsup on their paper plates. From somewhere came the smell of wood that was burning.